Fra

*dis***illus**

Frankly *dis*illusion*ed*

A True Saga of Mystery, Magic & Mayhem

by

Dean Metcalfe

The Cloister House Press

First published in the United Kingdom in 2013
by The Cloister House Press

ISBN 978–1–909465–04–6

For Claudine,
I could not have done this without you

And to my grandfather,
I guess one day all will become clear

Foreword

OVER THE YEARS we have laughed until we've cried, sharing the crazy stories of our travels as showbiz magicians. I have lost count of the times I've been asked to write about these experiences, but when you have so many stories it's hard to know where to start. I guess the simple solution to this is to start at the beginning! But my mind doesn't really work like that!

There's so much to tell you. And there are plenty of people along the way who influenced me, both in this world and the next (!) and who played a vital part in my very early days in magic. Not least my folks for buying me that first magic set – which of course was often what started many a young magician on the road to fame and fortune – or in my case, a life of mayhem and drama!

They say behind every successful man is a good woman. Well I'm still looking! Haha! (I will of course hide this bit from Claudine!)

All jokes aside though, I have no doubt that without Claudine by my side every step of the way, I would not have continued with a career in magic. I've been working now for 35 years, and still am. Even having to sit down and type this is something she would normally be doing – as I pace around the room dictating my words! She loves it though – just as she loves organising all our travel arrangements, while I am sitting by the fire waiting for my steak and chips to arrive! Well isn't that what a good assistant – sorry wife – is for?!

Even through many times of illness, Claudine has battled to be by my side – so the show could go on. (Probably afraid that I might otherwise have to hire another beautiful assistant!!) But she still tells me even now that she can take it or leave it – quite happy in the knowledge that she has been one of the very best – and certainly one of the most stunning and memorable magician's assistants in the world. So much so that I had critics saying that they didn't even notice me on stage when Claudine was there!

But it's all been worth it (I think). And to that end I would like say that this book is dedicated to my best friend and gorgeous wife, Claudine.

Chapter 1

RIGHT, HERE we go, I have no idea how to start this. Maybe I'll just sit here in this white chair. But I might make a cup of tea first. Yes. Good idea. I'll get a cup of tea.

Right. Okay then. People always ask me two things; how did I get into magic and does it run in the family – but I don't want to talk about those yet. Let me tell you about my weekend first; we were at a wedding at Dodford House in Northamptonshire – do you know it? Very nice place. I did a couple of hours of close-up magic, the guests were really enjoying it and the bride asked me to stay longer – but people don't understand that it takes it out of you sometimes, doing what I do. The adrenalin and trying to read your audience can be exhausting. But I did stay and it was a wonderful evening. But it was a classic example of how differently people react to magic. We were attempting to film some of my close-up magic for my website the next day in London, the film guys asked me to show some patrolling police officers some tricks, and they ran away! *Actually ran away*! I guess they didn't want to be filmed or they hated magic! Or both! Anyway, we can get back to that. I will tell you now about me as a boy. Oh, and by the way – the stories in this book are completely true – *every single one of them*. I can vouch for that – I was there!!

My father always told me to dream. Perhaps not what you expected me to say – but that was what he was like. He didn't say 'Dean, get a proper job' – not at all. Quite the opposite. My mother was a northern lass and I think had inherited a more down to earth and realistic approach to life. Good job really. But my father, he would say 'You've *got* to dream, but in a *massive* way.' He was an introverted man and always worked from home. He was a self-employed horse racing advisor and tipster; and as we all know with horse racing – you get your good bets and your bad bets. Money came in fast and went out faster. That was life. In those days it was all about the pools too; winning big on the pools. He didn't like the whole working nine-to-five for nothing thing. 'Dream big' he said. So I was fortunate really, in that I was encouraged to work hard, but also to never give up on my dreams.

Good thing really. Because all I did was dream about magic. I received a magic set for Christmas – I think I must have been about eight years old – and really and truly, from the moment I opened that box I was hooked. So I guess that's the answer to one of the two questions I'm often asked; how did I get into magic? Well, it started right there with me trying to work out the miracles in that magic box.

There was a joke shop in Beckenham, Kent, that sold magic. I literally used to spend all my pocket money in there! They sold those little tricks; the pretend Wrigley's chewing gum thing that half snapped your finger off – do you remember that? And itching powder? Always makes me laugh thinking about those little tricks. But I guess that was the start of it all. Any spare time or money I had, that's where I'd go. Oh, before I go on – you'll never believe this – I've got to tell you about the best trick of all they had! I don't know why I didn't get walloped really for this! They sold this book with a picture of a very sexy, voluptuous woman on the front – interesting for a 12 year old boy! It had a coil inside hooked up to a 9-volt battery – *a 9-volt* battery – you'd never get that now! Well, it had a metal band around the edge that gave you this big electric shock when you picked it up. You can't believe it can you?! A proper belt! I put it on the table near to my father's office in the house. Well, he came in the front door and down the hall to his office and oh boy, what a noise he made!! Can't believe it still makes me laugh, it was so long ago – but you should have heard him!

I often used to sneak off to London too. There was a magic department in Hamley's Toy Shop and quite often there'd be a magician doing some tricks there. There was this trick with a pack of cards, they were called the Svengali pack – still sold today – a very clever trick that ends with the whole pack becoming your card. I was so in awe of those tricks. I once plucked up courage to ask one of the magicians where else I could buy magic. He told me about a place in Holborn owned by a chap called Ron MacMillan. It was in Clerkenwell Road – can you believe it's actually still there! So I made my way across London, I was still only a kid, but found the place. There was a basement there where magicians would perform the sort of magic I'd only seen on TV. It was incredible and I would watch these guys in complete awe as they performed – as far as I was concerned – real, live miracles. I got to know some of the magicians and they would show me tricks that I could hardly believe. I realised I desperately needed to earn some more money to buy magic in that shop. But there was another reason too.

Not long after my first trip to the shop in Clerkenwell Road I met Henk Meesters, a slim, vain Dutch magician who was working at the International Magic Shop in London. He had very pale short hair and really blue eyes. He was hugely charismatic and very good-looking; a very seductive person, women loved him. European magic has always been more sophisticated and classy than British magic. It wasn't just about the big show of it all or just full of gags and jokes – it was as smooth as silk – classy and mesmerising; pure artistry. I'd never seen anything like it and I was spellbound. Henk saw something in me I think, aside from my enthusiasm; potential skill that I hadn't realised I even had – and offered to tutor me. I would regularly visit the apartment he was renting in London where I would spend hours and hours perfecting one slow flick of my wrist, or how to move a silk from one hand to another seamlessly, effortlessly. 'No,' he would say, 'Like this . . .' – showing me over and over and over. 'Hold your head like this, not like that. Stand tall. Show me your hands. Again. *Again*.' But this didn't come for free. Henk insisted I pay him. And quite rightly too.

So I got a job delivering meat for Wally, the butcher – hideous it was, really hard work. I had to deliver meat all over Beckenham – great, big posh houses some of them. Wally was a very skilled butcher and he had a huge amount of customers. The meat was wrapped in paper packets with hand-written labels tied on and I was given a tobacco tin of float. I had to load it all onto one of those trays on the front of a pushbike and ride up all these crazy hills. I'd knock on the huge front doors, starving hungry, and be greeted by – guess what – the smell of roast beef! I'd get a 20p tip sometimes and Wally would give me a piece of steak to take home. I lost the tobacco tin once though, and had to ride two miles back up the bloody hill to get it – I remembered that I'd left it on a wall – thankfully it was still there and with all the money still in it!

I think it was this year too that I went over to Spain on a school holiday and saw a magician performing magic in a club. He showed me some tricks too, with cigarettes, that were incredibly clever. And years later – with much practise – I eventually mastered the sleight of hand necessary to perform these amazing cigarette tricks. In fact, even now, they still remain some of my own personal favourites.

These were busy and exciting times for me between school and working and being tutored by Henk. I had so much energy. But the best bits were, by far, my visits to the professional magic shop in Holborn and seeing Henk. By now, as you've probably realised, I was completely and totally hooked on magic.

Chapter 2

HENK SUGGESTED I enter The Young Magician of the Year which was held at the famous Magic Circle, near Euston in London. I felt I was nowhere near ready, but Henk had no doubt that with his help I stood a chance of winning. He was a very confident man! He knew he was good! Nothing wrong with that. I was just 15 years old. I had no idea about nerves really, I just walked onto the stage of The Magic Circle for the very first time, and the hours spent with Henk perfecting the beautiful skills of manipulation paid off. The audience and the judges loved the fluidity of my young hands as I performed with large white thimbles and an ancient old illusion called The Chinese Rings – where the rings would, with the slightest of touches, link together. Magicians had rarely seen my slow and smooth style with the rings before, and my presentation was enormously successful. Finally, the winner was announced, 'And the winner of The Young Magician of the Year, 1977, is ... Dean Metcalfe ... and Russ Stevens!' That's right – we were joint winners! And rightly so. Russ presented an incredible act with doves – he was more commercial than me – and his act was quite fast and modern. Anyway, after our win Russ seemed to get more bookings than me, perhaps because of this very reason – whereas my act was more traditional and slower. I did buy some doves once – but turns out they were the wrong ones – these were white pigeons rather than the smaller Java doves that magicians use, so they were a bit on the big side for tricks! In fact I unwittingly put two males and a female together. This caused quite a stir really, because one of the male birds took to pecking the other on the head. It wasn't a pretty sight! However, I was at the time the youngest ever winner – and made sure everyone knew it – and I just remember feeling terribly excited! I didn't really know what was supposed to happen next.

After I won the Young Magician of the Year, I was invited by Ron MacMillan to perform in a magic gala in Holland. I would be joined by Henk and some other magicians. I was so young and my mind was full of magic. I remember all the sharp suits and the diamonds on the guys I met, friends of Ron's who owned The Van Moppes Diamond Factory in Amsterdam. And I remember also meeting so many other magicians and how shy I felt in front of them, but how much I loved being around them. Despite being so shy I was mature for my age, and my manipulation skills were already surprising magicians far older and more experienced than me. I was invited to perform at various magic galas and dinner dances where I was a huge success. It was an eye-opening experience watching the other magicians though – whose acts were often very elaborate. I was just worrying whether I could perform my thimble routine perfectly – the trick that consisted of me producing lots of thimbles on my fingertips – that would appear, of course, from nowhere! However, I became aware of this huge gulf between what they were doing compared to what I was just learning to do, and how much more I needed to include in my act to become more entertaining!

The Young Magician of The Year contest was televised on Blue Peter and people were starting to recognise me in the street. I thought up a name for myself and even had a designer create the artwork for me; 'Deano' – a hand with thimbles on each finger and the 'o' being a Chinese ring – it was really good, I was pretty proud of it. But Ron MacMillan later told me my stage name sounded a bit naff! Mother wanted me to use 'Ringo Thimble' – which, looking back, was quite funny! I paid a huge amount of money too for regular adverts in *The Stage and Television*, a theatrical newspaper – big, big adverts – talk about having an ego!

But if I imagined I would enter straight into the world of working as a full-time magician though, I was very wrong.

I left school the next year, when I was 15, and started work like everybody else. I had some awful jobs. One summer I worked at a holiday camp in Great Yarmouth. I hated it. 'You are the worst person I have *ever* seen do this job' the manager would shout at me. I couldn't disagree with him. I just couldn't keep that horrendous holiday camp malarkey up all day and all night for a minute longer. I thought I'd be doing magic – but I ended up having to do crap stuff like bloody showing the guests to their chalets and helping to prepare games with all the kids – it was hideous!

I returned to London. I started work for a travel agency just off Tower Bridge as a foot messenger, basically hand-delivering letters and plane tickets all over London. I loved it. I made a lot of extra money too. You may ask how on earth I managed to make this extra cash being a (notoriously poorly-paid) foot messenger. Here's how – (though perhaps I shouldn't be telling you this!); I was pretty fit physically, and delivering letters, etc all over London kept me in good shape. The girls at the desks would call me over, we'd have a bit of a banter and then they'd say 'Dean, deliver this to so-and-so' and 'that to such-and-such' and I'd wail 'I haven't got time to get all that done in one hour!' So they'd give me some money from petty cash and they'd book me a taxi ... which I er ... never used, well, occasionally I did – just for effect, you know. No, I had no use for taxis – I'd run and just keep the cash! I'd leg it all through the back streets and alleyways of London, making all my deliveries. I never missed a single one. Then I'd wipe the sweat off my brow, catch my breath, and walk back into the office and hand them the receipt for the taxi I'd never used. So how, you may ask, did I get hold of the receipts? Easy; on the occasions I did use the taxi, I got the driver to hand me a bunch of receipts, saying that it would save time for next time, and fill them in myself. What can I say?

There's one delivery I'll never forget though. I was used to meeting all these posh ladies in smart houses and beautiful clothes, but one time I remember going up to the door of this massive house in Belgravia; a huge, great, shiny, black door with pillars on each side. The lady asked me to step inside for a moment. And would you believe it – there was a huge, circular fish pond built into the marble floor in the middle of the colossal lounge, all lit up from underneath. I remember two things about that; the sound of her high heels as she walked across the marble floor and thinking, 'This is another world.' In my street, people brandished screwdrivers and took each other out with imaginary machine guns!

The old boys in the post rooms too, they were great – they couldn't wait to see some of my latest tricks – so I always made sure I had something up my sleeve as it were! It was a good test for me.

So then, I was still doing magic – not just for the old boys of course – but mainly for Magicians' galas. On one such occasion I was asked to close the evening with some magic. Little did I know, but Edwin Hooper, owner of The Supreme Magic Company – the biggest magic company in the world (but incredibly he was based in the small town of Bideford in Devon) – was in the audience. I performed a trick that involved lowering a lit candelabra into a brown paper bag, causing it to disappear whilst simultaneously extinguishing the flame. I have to explain that the candelabra and candle are made of a very soft, collapsible rubber that has to be handled with extreme skill so as to appear solid. So there I stood, having made a lovely show of lighting and smoking a cigarette from the candle flame, and then all eyes were on the flaming candelabra as it descended into the paper bag. The bag is then crushed (and the flame extinguished) with a dramatic clap and bang of the hands and hurled into the darkness at the back of the stage – to rapturous applause. Well, that's how it's supposed to end ... For some reason I glanced behind me, distracted by a rustling noise. To my absolute horror the bag had started to unravel and the candle was slowly emerging from it as if having taken on a life of its own! I was absolutely furious. I had no idea what to do. So I just walked around and kicked the bag into the audience with all of my might! What a thing to do! Well, the audience collapsed into hysterics. I really do not know how I managed to finish my act.

I eventually stormed off stage and down the corridor into my dressing room, slamming the door. I was mortified, I'd never had anything go wrong before. Who should appear a few minutes later, but Edwin Hooper, who proceeded to laugh his head off – claiming he had never seen anything so wonderfully funny. His acceptance and humour about what had seemed to me like the end of the world calmed me down and I laughed too – although I was still bloody gutted! In later years Edwin proved to be a good friend, and on many occasions I was invited to demonstrate magic and perform at the magic conventions he would put on around the country.

Magic is a strange world. Up one minute, down the next. You're 'The best thing since Paul Daniels' one week, but you're 'Not as good as Dynamo' the next. Even now the reactions to what I do are quite unpredictable. Going back to when we were trying to put together that short bit of film in London for my website, the reactions to my close-up magic were pretty erratic. From the police officers who ran away so fast you'd think I was going to put a voodoo spell on them or something, to the girls wearing next-to-nothing who took to screaming 'Oh my God, Oh my God, Oh my God, pick me, pick me!! I wanna see the magic!!' when they found out what I was doing – it was all just so . . . strange – for want of a better word. Then there was the guy who insisted on showing *me* a trick. A great, big seven-foot (well, seemed like it at the time – he was certainly a lot taller than me – which is not difficult!) tattooed, bald chunk of beer/drug induced adrenalin who shouted louder and louder as he attempted to – unsuccessfully – perform his trick for me. He then turned around and punched the guy behind him in the head, then wandered off. Bizarre!

Later on, in a rather classy club in Hyde Park, I was doing a bit of magic for some of the people in there. I think at this point we'd given up attempting to film. After a while a rather elderly, but beautifully attired and well-spoken lady came over to me, took me by the arm and pronounced, 'I don't know why you want to do magic here, dear, this is just a posh mating club.' About says it all really.

I appeared with Paul Daniels on a Saturday morning TV show immediately after winning Young Magician of the Year. I recall he wasn't particularly welcoming when I was at the TV studio, in fact I'd go so far as to say that he was just an intsy-tintsy bit jealous of the attention I was getting. I learned that he had gained a reputation for not being very kind to younger magicians. There was also in later years, bad blood between him and the press concerning a fantastically talented up-and-coming star by the name of Wayne Dobson. At the time I assumed this was just the press typically turning rumour into fact, but by all accounts it was absolutely true. Wayne Dobson is a truly nice guy, who sadly developed multiple sclerosis at the height of his career. He is in a wheelchair now but still hugely admired, especially by magicians, for his sheer brilliance. He sells magic and still comes up with amazing new ideas; a great, great guy.

Another magician who became a friend at this time was a chap called Tony Corinda. In earlier years he had run his own magic studio in London, and later manned the magic concession in Hamley's. He wrote this wonderful book for magicians called '13 Steps to Mentalism!' This book teaches the sort of things you have seen Derren Brown present. I'm not saying that I knew Tony very well, but I would sometimes pop around to his big house in Hemel Hempstead. By all appearances he was doing pretty well for himself – but you can never really tell, can you!? I just remember him being such an absolute character – dominating dinner parties with his total madness. Do you remember those joke credit cards that were sold in novelty shops? They had ridiculous things printed on them like, 'Sorry I was late, I was run over by a herd of elephants' – well, Tony invented those and that was Tony all over. I once invited Tony over to Anerley to meet my parents in our humble house in Thornsett Road. My mother prepared a meal for us and the first thing he said to her was, 'Whenever I come over the river from north to south, I feel like throwing buns to everyone!' Can you believe that?! Not a good start. My mother resented him forever. But it still makes me laugh!

Just 15 years old back home with my Young Magician of The Year Award, 1977

And here with the ancient Chinese Linking Rings which won me the above award

Chapter 3

But my parents do laugh, and so do I, when we remember one trick that I was desperately trying to perfect when I was a young boy. And I think it's fair to say that I don't think our Collie dog, Lucky, ever recovered. I was in my bedroom with the door open trying over and over to do this trick that simply involved lowering a very slim walking cane into a pot on the floor. Done correctly, the cane would then instantaneously turn into a large and very colourful bouquet of flowers. Do you think I could do it? I tried and tried. Lucky was watching most curiously from the doorway. I don't know what he thought I was doing, but he was completely rapt. I was just beginning to lose patience, when *bang!* Suddenly the cane obediently and dramatically transformed itself into the required bunch of flowers! I was so happy! Lucky on the other hand, clearly thought it was the most terrifying thing he had ever seen, jumped three feet in the air and threw himself down the hallway barking hysterically! He never returned to my room again.

What people may or may not realise about magic is that it has to be delivered. There has to be such control and fluidity to the movements. And this is why I would spend so long perfecting even the simplest trick – it had to be fluid and appear effortless. Everything these days seems to be about the bang and crash of it all, huge, loud statement acts that are all for effect. And television is all about the editing. Audience reactions are monitored closely and then clipped to suit. TV magic is a very different world – but more on that later! To perform *live* in cabaret shows is a skill in a league of its own.

When I was starting out, I was always slightly shocked by people's reactions to magic, especially in London. As you know, I still am! 'Show us a fuckin' trick then mate, come on – show us a fuckin' trick,' blokes would shout. So I'd show them something and then they'd yell, 'But where's ya bird, mate – if ya gonna do magic you gotta 'av a fuckin' bird wiv ya! And if you wanna be a great magician you gotta to do the *big stuff* like sawing people in 'alf!' Or women would get all ridiculous and start mauling me – magic *can be* sexy, but I didn't consider myself like that – but they'd be like 'Ooooh, it turns me on . . .' Crazy talk like that.

I loved watching David Nixon. He was a member of The Magic Circle and his presence on TV was unforgettable. I think everyone of a certain age remembers him, he had such a wonderful, warm personality and at the peak of his career was the UK's most famous magician. Paul Daniels too – obviously I remember watching him – long before I met him. He used a lot more humour with his magic, but was hugely entertaining. Those two guys had a huge influence on me. This brings me to the point where I answer the second of the most commonly asked questions (and *the* one that I always try to avoid!); 'Was I influenced in any way by a *family* member who was into magic, or in other words, did magic run in the family?' Okay. Here we go . . .

My grandfather, on my father's side, was a very interesting person; a stage performer who went by the name of Jagana. He described himself as a clairvoyant, a foreseer of events and a mind-reader. It's fair and obvious to say that I may have inherited his passion for the magical and the mysterious. But I don't ever recall meeting him in person.

My grandfather was very much in demand in the 1940s. These were the days when variety shows were hugely popular. He used to book other acts too and I still have letters from the likes of Tommy Trinder and Max Bygraves thanking him for his bookings. The Queen Mother too sent him a letter of gratitude for a lucky mascot he sent her which he called 'The Amen-Ra.' I wish however, that it were that simple, and this is part of the reason why I try to avoid this particular question. Because, yes, later in life my grandfather did have an influence on me. But the truth is – it wasn't always a positive thing. That might sound in itself quite an odd statement; it depends upon your feelings about what I'm about to say next.

You see, my grandfather committed suicide, and I feel that as a very young child, about five years old at the time, this was something I wasn't really ever supposed to know about or understand. It's not a time I remember an awful lot about or even thought about – until I got into magic – and then many strange and spooky things started to happen to me. Too many things, in the end, to be ignored as coincidence. And those things I do remember, in fact it is completely impossible to forget them. So, whether I like it or not, my grandfather did indeed greatly influence me, but only after he died . . .

But I have always been fascinated by my grandfather's life in magic and his achievements – despite the fact that his influence on me has sometimes felt very negative. There are stories I will tell you that will send shivers up your spine. Here is one of them. When I say that I don't remember very much from around the time that he killed himself, this is true – but one thing is seared into my memory. The house that day had a terrible feel to it. I was so young, but I distinctly remember the heaviness and oppression. I left my room and walked to the kitchen. My mother was standing at the kitchen sink her head down, staring into the water. She was silhouetted by the window and she was standing very still. I stood in the doorway, not making a sound, not wishing to disturb her. There were several things on the drainer and for some reason my eyes became fixed on the large brandy glass that was drying there. I tried to turn away from it, sensing something that I didn't understand. Another second passed and then the brandy glass suddenly exploded, sending shards of glass high into the air. I didn't stay to see my mother's reaction – I ran back to my own room and closed the door. I'd seen enough.

Perhaps one of the other reasons I have always avoided this question is that I felt that people would instantly associate my success with that of my grandfather's if they knew of his history. I wanted to be acclaimed on my own merit, and not have to carry that with me. Is that wrong? I don't know. Maybe that's why I've always felt this undercurrent, this ominous presence. Was I in some way denying his existence by deliberately not talking about him? Is that why he still had to make his presence felt in my life?

Just the other day, I was sitting in my office chatting to a friend. She suddenly stopped talking mid-sentence and glanced behind her, looking bemused. She took in the tightly shut double-glazed window; the closed door; where I was sitting and where she was sitting. 'Someone's smoking,' she said, gesturing, 'someone just walked from there to there smoking a really strong cigarette.' I couldn't really do anything else except smile and explain, we had been discussing my grandfather after all, who had been a heavy smoker. Thankfully she has an open mind and just accepted this, and we continued our conversation.

So there it is really, my early beginnings in magic. And the reason for my avoidance of one of the two questions that I am always asked. There is so much more to tell you. Penniless months and months on the road across Europe; sharing rooms with rats one minute and the stage with celebrities the next; meeting the 'bird' that would change my whole life – and hers. But you know what, I wouldn't change a thing, not for a minute – except perhaps … no – that'll have to wait. I'll tell you about the crazy road I lived on first, if that's okay.

Chapter 4

SO. THORNSETT ROAD. This is in a place called Anerley – sandwiched between Penge and South Norwood in London. SE20 to be precise. This is where I grew up. What a place.

There weren't half some characters in my road. There was this really tall, youngish sort of chap who looked a bit demented really, if I'm honest. I don't know why but he was the guy who often had a large screwdriver in his hand and I'm pretty sure it had some red stuff on the end (but I was a highly imaginative kid!). He'd stand in his front garden and threaten us and then make this mock attempt at charging at us – it was mad – but we were kids so we could leg it pretty fast to get away from him!

Then there was this other bloke who lived on one side of us – again, really tall – like seriously about six-and-a-half feet tall! He took huge strides when he was walking, he was the quickest person I'd ever seen – I would try to keep up with him, having to run obviously, and chase him up the street. Other times we would be playing out in the street, my brother and me and some mates, pretending to shoot each other with toy guns – and he would join in – I mean *really* join in. He would seriously get into it – firing semi-automatic machine guns, making all the noises and everything, even miming the actions of taking the pin out of a hand grenade and chucking it at us! We realised much later that he had been in the Forces. He wasn't playing in the sense that we were playing. Not at all. He'd seen real action and was suffering from shellshock, or similar, poor man. We'd often see him through our side window, stamping and marching and saluting, shouting at the top of his voice 'Stand to attention!'

Not everybody wielded screwdrivers or chucked imaginary hand grenades though. Thomas Crapper at one time lived at one end of the street, famous inventor of the lavatory flushing system, as we all know. Useful bloke. Next door used to belong to the poet, Walter de la Mare, who also penned several psychological horror stories. Opposite were a Mr and Mrs Fisher who occasionally appeared on TV discussing education and schooling (not one of my most favourite subjects!). We also had producers for Top of the Pops further along the road and the famous watchmaker, George Daniels too. He was a strange chap, a bit of a recluse, as they say. We all knew his house but we never saw him. He did come out for the 1977 Silver Jubilee celebrations though. We had a huge street party and I remember he was really pleasant to me. I had some coins with holes in; I was doing some tricks with them. He asked me if I knew why they had holes – I didn't – so he explained that it was to save money when they were being made. Funny the things you remember.

I remember that I used to keep all my magic locked up in a cabinet. My younger brother, Ray, wasn't interested in magic – but he was very interested in annoying me by finding out how it was done! I reckon he's still the same now! The other day he reminded me how I used to set up trip wires and booby traps in my bedroom to protect my tricks. One thing I used to do was glue two or three hairs along the middle of where the two doors to my magic cabinet joined up – you obviously couldn't see the hairs unless you looked really closely. And if ever I saw that those hairs were broken – then war would begin!!

I also remember performing 'magic shows' for my parents and my brother – always at the wrong time of course, like in the middle of a feature film or when my father was busy working in his office. There was always some kind of failure (I'm laughing now!) – and as you know – I didn't handle things going wrong very well! Or the door bell would go, or the telephone would ring – just before my grand finale. Or my brother would shout constantly 'I know how it's done, I know how it's done . . .!' I really hated them all then!

I'd storm off and go fishing, I loved fishing and never cared what the weather was like in those days. There were a couple of lakes in Norwood and Crystal Palace, I could calm down by the sides of those lakes. I don't fish now – not unless it's a lovely day – I've gone soft in my old age! I was seriously into cycling too and won several medals for racing. Believe it or not I used to belong to a cycling club called the Dulwich Paragon and I would race in competitions at Crystal Palace. I don't race anymore – but I still have a racing bike and I'll take it out when I find the time – providing the weather is okay!

Lots of things change when we get older, for some reason we don't remember the same sorts of things as when we were kids, or else we just see them differently. I've lived in so many places, but my memories of those people in Thornsett Road are some of the most vivid I have. I'll tell you about some of the places I've lived though – total shit holes! And some of the shit jobs I've done for shit money and the shitty trains that never came on time to take me to the shit jobs that paid shit money. That's a whole lot of shit to discuss!!

Chapter 5

I HAVE TO ADMIT that I probably inherited my rather negative attitude towards regular day jobs from my father. All those years of him yelling, 'You don't want to be like everyone else, working for nothing. There's more to life, you know!' I'd only just won The Young Magician of the Year, and those rants didn't really help my ego – I already thought everything else was beneath me. I shouldn't really have been thinking like that at all. But it was a benefit to me in one way – because it gave me the drive and the ambition to never give up on my dream of making a living out of magic. I had no idea it would take nine years to make this dream real. Good job I didn't know then about all the crap jobs and late trains ahead of me! I might have lost the plot completely!

God, trains. We lived about a 20-minute walk away from Norwood Junction Station. I didn't mind that so much, it was what invariably happened next that used to piss me off. The trains rarely came on time – what are the stats now on trains arriving on time – something like 88 percent of the time? – well back then it was zilch percent of the time. So I'd either miss the one that was supposed to be on time but had been late, i.e. arriving at 7:30am instead of 7:00am or wait half an hour for the next one because it was running late, only to miss it because I was a minute too late, or early, or whatever. I know that makes no sense whatsoever. Neither did the trains. So anyway, I'd eventually catch a train into Central London, because that's where all the jobs were that I did. I'd sit or stand crammed between anyone from a really nice suited gentleman reading a newspaper that took up two seats to a really smelly person with bad breath who wanted to talk to me, or some weirdo humming to himself. Then I'd have to get on a tube train wedged between an equally diverse cross-section of society, to finally arrive at a job I really hated. Which reminds me of the last time I ever saw Henk – we were on a tube train together – but I'll tell you about that in a minute.

And God, the jobs. Jobs in jewellers, fashion stores, stationers, department stores. Jobs all over the place. All with really shit money and very few laughs. None of them lasted very long. All I cared about was getting to the end of the week, getting paid and paying for my next advertisement in *The Stage and Television*, and buying magic for my next performance.

By now I was about 18 years old and in the early 80s discos were really starting to be *the* place to go. Oh wait, sorry, meant to tell you about Henk and the tube journey. We'll get back to discos later.

As you know, Henk tutored me to the point where I won The Young Magician of the Year and that I paid him for this. I wasn't quite sure what was supposed to happen next, but shortly after I was talking to Ron MacMillan, the owner of the magic shop in Clerkenwell Road. He was a member of the Freemasons and invited me to do some magic after one of their meetings in a location, that in honour of true Freemason tradition, will remain undisclosed. So off I went with Ron, to arrive at a rather grand place, where I was asked to sit in a large, well-furnished side room while they conducted their meeting. I wasn't being paid for this, I'd been invited purely on the merit of my magic by Ron, who thought that it would be an interesting experience for me. Well eventually these tall, heavily carved, double doors opened and I was invited into the room. All eyes were on me from both sides of a very long and highly-polished mahogany table. I performed some magic, nervously at first, and then with more confidence as I warmed to my most curious audience and they warmed to me. They were impressed, I have to say, and applauded me! Ron explained a little about me, adding that I had, for their benefit, performed for free that night. So, and this is no joke, they found a bottle which they passed around the table and then to me. As the bottle went from hand-to-hand, each gentleman put some cash into it. The evening came to an end and I went home clutching my bottle of cash. I sat on my bed and emptied out the contents. There was £27 in that bottle! I couldn't believe it! It took me *days* to earn £27 in my little part-time jobs!

I saw Henk a few days later; we were taking a tube ride back from someplace or other. I told him, very excitedly, about my evening with the Freemasons and the bottle with the £27 in it. We must have looked an interesting pair, Henk and me, because all the weird and wonderful people sat around us on the tube train kept shooting us sideways glances; this short, dark-haired excitable boy sat opposite a tall, refined Dutchman talking about magic, Freemasons and bottles of cash. Well, Henk listened and then he fixed me with his blue eyes, and very calmly asked me for his commission. As far as I was concerned I didn't owe him any commission, and said so, explaining that the evening had been organised by Ron MacMillan and hadn't got anything to do with Henk. He never said a word, just looked away. We arrived at our stop and got off the train. He simply walked off into the crowd and that was that. I never saw him again.

Chapter 6

I MUST TELL YOU a funny story about a trip we made through France and Belgium. It's only short but still makes me laugh when I think about it, then I'll tell you about my cruise ship antics! We were going through customs into Belgium and had a suitcase of ... let me rewind, or this won't make sense. We have this trick that we conjurors do with these little foam balls. We place a single foam ball in your hand (or so you think) and ask you to squeeze it really tight. Thing is, we haven't just put one ball in your hand – we've put several – because we're magicians right, and we're really clever. So we ask you to squeeze really hard and then release your hand suddenly, opening it wide. You expect to see one little ball in your hand – or maybe that it has disappeared. But these balls have the capacity to expand to many times their own size and are made of a compound that makes them take off at great speed of their own free will ... a totally harmless but quite amusing little trick. Well, we get pulled over at customs and we had a great big suitcase of the things in the boot, and guess what? The customs officers want to know what's in the case. So with no more than a sly little glance at each other ... we stand back and allow them to open the suitcase. Being the big, tough customs guys that they are of course, they throw the suitcase open, expecting weapons, drugs, body parts or God knows what else ... and literally hundreds of the things launch themselves out of the case in a hundred different directions! Guess you weren't expecting that guys!! Well we thought it was funny.

Let me tell you now about my first cruise contract. Al Heath called me. Al was a very established entertainment agent in the 1980s. He had a booking for a magician on a 5-star cruise ship with Royal Viking Lines (owned by Cunard). As you can imagine I was very excited at the thought of performing on a cruise ship and even more excited when I was given the contract. But my excitement turned to horror when I realised what I had signed for. Rule number one; *always* read *all* of the contract (not just the first ten lines that tell you what you'll be paid – which in this case was many times my regular weekly salary!). What's that saying? 'The first 10 minutes of an offer are always the most exciting' – before, sometime later, you get hit with the stark realisation of what you've agreed to!

So off I went down to Southampton to join my first cruise ship. It was 1980 and I was only 18 years old and totally awestruck by the beauty and sheer class of it all. The ship was absolutely stunning. My father drove me down there and made all the usual jokes of hiding in my suitcase, etc, etc. The cruise director was a man called Ray Avon and he called a meeting for all the entertainers as soon as the ship departed. The meeting was very professional, and I realised immediately that all the other entertainers were a lot older and wiser than me and very seasoned performers. I felt suddenly daunted by this and also by the fact that I didn't feel at all connected with any of them on a social level. And then came the shock; Ray went on to discuss the itinerary of each act. It never occurred to me that I would be expected to perform more than about 15 minutes of magic (*always* read *all* the contract ...), but I was wrong. I was required to perform two acts lasting 15 minutes each plus and an extra five minutes for the farewell show – it was material I simply did not have! This was the rather important detail on the contract that I had not read – I'd just spotted the bit with the '£' signs. Sounds nuts, but to be honest, I wasn't massively worried for some reason – I just felt like I was on holiday. And I was more interested by that point in heading down to one of the ship's restaurants to sample the food.

And enjoy the food I did; lobster, fillet steak and midnight buffets. I rather liked lying in the sunshine by the pool in the day, watching the beautiful Mediterranean pass by. This was a very high class ship, and in those days entertainers were treated like passengers; every wish was catered for. I loved the way everybody dressed for dinner, in ball gowns and tuxedos. It was sheer luxury and I couldn't believe the way my life was turning out. What could go wrong?

But after a couple of days I was getting restless. 'Time for a practical joke' I think to myself . . . little did I know this might signal the beginning of the end for my days on this cruise ship!

I had this magic two-pence piece that had the tiniest hole drilled in the middle of one side, so that on that side it looked completely normal. The coin however had been drilled out so that it was, in fact, hollow inside and the other side had a dome-shaped, wafer-thin layer of alloy. This means that you can do marvellous things with this coin. One of the things you can do is to get this seemingly completely 'normal' two-pence piece to leap several feet in the air without any *help* whatsoever! This is done by pushing in the alloy dome and slowly rubbing it with your fingers (in an almost indiscernible manner). It then warms up allowing the coin to lie totally flat on a table like all other coins. But it has been heated, so as it cools, the alloy dome pops out – launching the coin into mid-air. This was relatively amusing, but not the most humorous thing this coin could do.

Remember that this coin also had the finest hole drilled in it too. If you submerged it in water (with the alloy part of the coin pushed in) and then released the alloy – it would suck in the water. But if you depressed the alloy it would send out a sudden, and quite fierce, jet of water at an unsuspecting victim.

Well, having the fidgets, I decided to roam about the ship and try this new trick on someone for the first time. It wasn't long before I spotted two rather glamorous older ladies, all beautifully made-up for dinner in fine dresses and full make-up, clearly quite wealthy. As they drew closer I realised that they were American – not that this makes what I did to them remotely more acceptable, okay! So anyway, with all the bravado that I could muster, I went up to them and asked them if they had seen any of our English coins close-up, or something like that. They looked a bit perplexed, so I blundered on – asking them if they'd noticed that our Queen's head appears on coins of even the smallest denomination, like the two-pence piece. I knew that being American they would love that; Americans love our Monarchy. So the one lady, curious now, removes her gold-rimmed glasses and peers down her nose to have a closer look at our lovely Queen on the coin. It was at this point, obviously, that I deployed the alloy at the back of the coin and bulls eye! I shoot a fast and powerful fine jet of water straight into the middle of her eye! After a couple of seconds I realise I'm not quite getting the reaction that I hoped – the lady had her hand over her eye and was gasping and moaning, she grabs hold of the banister of the hallway and slowly slides to the floor. Her mascara is running down her face and she is by now cursing me too. I offer her my handkerchief, which I thought was quite manly, but she got to her feet and clutching her friend, staggered off down the corridor. I just shrugged and imagined that that was that really ... or so I thought. Anyhow, I had a performance that night, so I wandered off backstage to prepare.

The next night I had to come up with a bit more material, as the rota had been changed at the last minute. So I devised another trick with the Chinese linking rings that I had used the night before. It went like this; I invited a victim, sorry *volunteer*, onto the stage. I describe how the volunteer will help me with this trick, and in addition explain to the audience that the trick I am going to show them will give them a little glimpse of how magic is done. This is to help the audience to appreciate the skills a magician uses and to build anticipation for the act. So this lady joins me on stage to help me demonstrate the trick. She sits down on a little stool and I ask her to clasp her hands tightly together and put her elbows on her knees. I then explain that I will have to blindfold her and proceed in tying a piece of silk tightly over her eyes and face, knotting it at the back of her head. All is going well. I then go on to say that I will touch her legs, arm and back with the single chromed Chinese ring. The basic gist of the trick is at one point I get the woman to take hold of the ring – but I slip a second ring over the arm of my volunteer at the same time – impossible of course since her hands have been very tightly clasped. Problem was, the audience were not really that impressed because it's complicated to follow and even worse to try and explain here! I was getting flustered trying to juggle several rings and a microphone and worse still, the lady who had volunteered started swaying on the stool. She had muttered something to me a few minutes before as I had tied the scarf around her face, but in my battle of trying to handle everything I had ignored her. Turns out I had tied the scarf so tightly and wedged it under her nostrils – so she was struggling to breathe, and was starting to panic – so I rush to complete the trick and quickly remove the blindfold. She jumps up and runs back to her seat spluttering and coughing ... to absolute silence from the audience – a performer's nightmare – and I beat a hasty retreat from the stage. Years later I still reflect on this experience. Even the simplest of tricks must be rehearsed thoroughly, so that any unexpected pitfalls in a live performance can be ironed out immediately and professionally – so as not to affect the act or the audience – or your victim! Something I learned the hard way on quite a number of occasions!

In my naivety though I'm pretty sure I'm still making a great impression on the cruise ship and I'm happy about that. 'I am big news on this ship,' I think. So I'm standing buying a Mars Bar from a small kiosk (I'm getting sick of posh food!) when there is a tap on my shoulder. Well I turn around and who is there but, and you have to believe this, the lady I nearly suffocated on stage the night before and the lady I squirted in the eye with water from my trick coin. And they're really not happy. They're both talking at once and it's quite threatening. The suffocated lady was pointing at the eye of the squirted lady and to my horror, her eye was all black and yellow and infected. It hadn't occurred to me to wash the inside of the coin and quite a bit of muck and debris had landed in her eye. Ooops! But it wasn't all bad news as far as I was concerned – apparently everybody was talking about what I would be doing for the farewell show in four days' time. Little did they, or I, know quite what a finale that would be ...

The next few days were just one big holiday really; relaxing in the sun and eating good food. I did get the feeling that the other entertainers didn't really want much to do with me, but I wasn't really that bothered; I was too busy enjoying myself and planning my final act.

There is an ancient and wonderful illusion that we magicians call The Floating Zombie or Sacred Sun Ball. It involves a highly polished aluminium ball that seemingly floats by itself around a silk cloth. In the right hands it is a really beautiful illusion, and I had become very adept at performing this. In later years it would go on to become a favourite part of my shows and I even went on to make videos teaching other magicians how to perfect this illusion. But these, remember, were my formative years and I felt I wanted to add something a bit more unique to this trick. So I decide that when the ball comes to rest on its pedestal at the end of the illusion I would throw the cloth in the air – to show that there are no wires attached – and then I would pull the ball apart holding two halves. Inside I would use magician's flash paper wrapped around a smoke capsule and ignite the contents inside the ball and thus end the act in a brilliant and dramatic flash of flame and ball of smoke. This, I am sure, would enhance the end of the show and my act considerably. I was already the talk of the ship (!) and this would make sure, once and for all, that they wouldn't forget me. And boy oh boy – they were sure to never forget me!

Thing is, despite my rule of always rehearsing everything, I hadn't experimented with how much of the chalk-like stuff I needed to use in the ball to get the effect I needed. Builders use these smoke capsules to check for leaks and draw in chimneys, so I just bunged a load into the ball and began my act. Let's just say I probably used about 50 times more than I actually needed. The smoke just kept pouring out, tonnes of it – the air-conditioning was drawing it into the room – and within 30 seconds the room was completely full of thick smoke that set all the smoke alarms off. People were screaming and shouting 'Is it poisonous, is it poisonous?!?' They fled the room and that was it . . . the end of my act and the end of my first week on a cruise ship.

I rang the agents several times asking if they had any work for me, but they always said they were fully booked and didn't have any vacancies for me in the foreseeable future.

Years later, when I went on to perform on cruise ships with my wife (must tell you about my wife . . .), I made sure people remembered my acts for the right reasons and not because they'd been half-blinded, suffocated or gassed!

Chapter 7

I RETURNED TO THE UK after my lovely cruise, and started looking around again for work. This is where we come back to discos! Discos were really becoming popular and there were loads of clubs springing up all over the UK in the early 80s, with some really good ones in London like Zenon's in Piccadilly and The London Hippodrome. They often had large stages and fantastic lighting – so I thought I would try out my talents at some of these venues. The problem I had though was that the act I had used to win The Young Magician of the Year; the gentle and very skilled manipulation of thimbles and the Chinese linking rings, simply didn't have any effect in these clubs. To be honest with you, looking back, I think the girls and guys – who all seemed so much older than me and certainly drunker – wanted something a little bit more dramatic and exciting, if at all! I think they were looking for something entirely different if you know what I mean! To quote the wonderful lady in the club in Hyde Park over 30 years later; 'I don't know why you want to do magic here, dear, this is just a (not so!) posh mating club!!' Nothing really changes at all does it! I wonder what people will be doing in another 30 years' time?!

There were a few acts though that were hugely successful. There were sexy troupes of girls that would perform very raunchy dancing and stuff with whips and suspenders and all dressed in leather. Not surprisingly they were very popular! I rather liked them myself!! And there was this guy call Stevie Starr who would regurgitate coins and fish – amazing he was. He's still performing now and he's very good. In fact I was always really envious of his act – he would arrive with hardly any props – well apart from the coins and the fish. Not forgetting also, in complete contrast, the performer whose main prop was a coffin on stage. He would use the music from Michael Jackson's Thriller and would suddenly sit bolt upright in the coffin in a fantastic zombie costume and all this brilliant make-up. He would then climb out of the coffin and dance as he began his act; he was the most incredible dancer. His finale was to produce this huge piece of *liver* from his mouth, with blood dripping down his front – all the girls would scream and completely freak out! But that's what they wanted in discos in those days.

I learned a lot from watching these guys though. I starting adding much more exciting elements into my act, like flames and fire, and my act was backed by proper disco music. And although I didn't get the best contracts – the bookings started coming in. But, as with most things, the popularity of entertainment acts in discos started to wane and I began to look for other work.

Around this time, circa 1982, I entered one of the largest magic competitions in Europe; the International Brotherhood of Magician's Contest in Great Yarmouth. This contest was made up of various categories, for example; stage/originality/manipulation etc, and as a competitor you decide which category you think you have best chance in winning. I decided to enter the manipulation category, so I filled out the form. I came up with an idea to use coins in my act – as there is this well-known magical effect that we magicians call the Meiser's Dream – I decided to use that. This is what happens; we make an elaborate show of displaying our empty hands – only to pluck coin after coin from the air – normally dropping them into something like a champagne bucket, which creates a loud noise for extra effect. Anyway, I worked on a unique way to produce a very large quantity of coins – which I'm not going to reveal to you! But it fooled my fellow peers and together with my other manipulations with the thimbles, I took first prize – The Dittia Shield. By this time though I wasn't hell-bent on just winning more magical awards – I'd developed a taste for working commercially – which was more important to me than just pleasing magicians.

It was then that, most mysteriously, another 'Henk' suddenly turned up in my life – this time Henk Vermeiden. He'd seen me perform at this competition. Henk Vermeiden was a hugely respected impresario and also from Holland. He was a world-respected figure within the magic community since he had both influenced, and taught, magical presentations for the stage to world champions of magic – and he wanted me to go over to Holland to learn further skills with him. But at a price. It was an honour of course to be asked, and other well-known magicians said I should jump at the chance – which I did. However, I had to first convince my parents – who would have to come up with the £500 for the trip (which in those days was a lot of money!) – and all for just a couple of weeks tuition. In the end, they agreed to me making the trip and found the money from somewhere. I was thrilled and I was sure that I would come back with a whole new sensational act. (I know for sure that my folks were expecting this after forking out this amount of money!) Instead, all I really came back with was the ability to pick up a silk gracefully! So nobody *in the whole world* can do this like me now! But for £500 – who wants to! All jokes aside though, my time with Henk wasn't wasted; presentation is *everything* and my stay with him only confirmed this. My belief about *how* magic should be presented was now totally reinforced. These days lots of magicians, especially those from countries like Japan and Korea, have their own unique way of performing. And in their case it's normally as fast as lightening – so different from my way of performing – which is about making it smooth and deliberate and indeed, beautiful to watch.

So for the next year or so, life was all about looking for the next big contract, but also finding one night bookings to keep me going. I would always pick up my copy of *The Stage* first thing on a Thursday morning, pouring over it looking for anything new or different. It was on one such Thursday that I spotted the advert that would change my life. A producer in Jersey was looking for acts for the summer season. I went for it. And boy did my life change.

Here's that floating ball that caused the mayhem with all that smoke on my first cruise ship contract

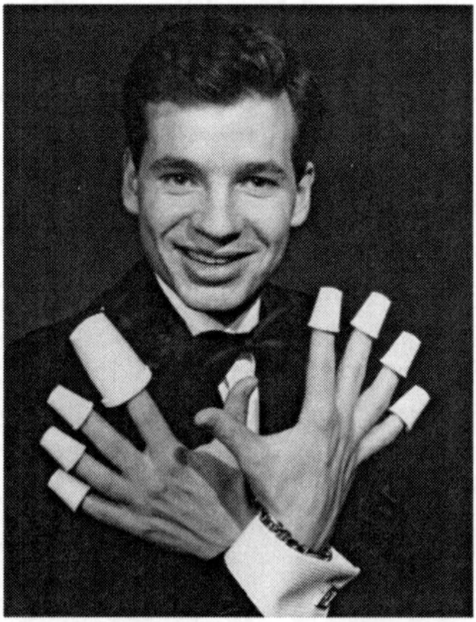

My prize-winning manipulating thimbles routine

Chapter 8

It was by now early 1985 and I was invited, along with other acts, to an audition in London for the job in Jersey. My spot was to be 10 minutes. It was a very brightly lit studio – not ideal at all for my act – and after just three minutes I was stopped. I held my breath. But I was then told I had got the job. At this point however, I was holding a sort of fan of live flames, that I had magically produced from absolutely nowhere of course – well not really, but you know what I mean! Each flame was pretty fierce – at least two feet high. I had been at the point, equally as magically, where I was about to dramatically extinguish the fire by pushing the fan into a slim box that would suffocate the flames. So there I was, two-foot flames pouring from the fan effect on the ends of my fingers, when not only was I stopped – but I also realised I hadn't prepared the box!! Running from the stage I spotted the nearest toilet, thankfully the gents, and threw the door open. The toilet was rather dimly lit, most of the bulbs had blown, and there was this guy having a pee at the far end in front of a very large mirror. You can imagine the look on his face when he saw me come flying through the door in the reflection in the mirror – to all appearances – on fire! He literally screeched, pissed all over his trousers and ran out – just as I managed to extinguish the flames with water in the sink.

Upon returning to the studio, having narrowly avoided setting fire to the stage, myself and probably the whole building – it was again confirmed that I had the job. There was no mention of money though. Turns out it was shit – no more than a normal wage for a person my age in the early 80s – about £160 a week, and I had to find my own accommodation. I was expecting great money too! But no matter, I was just happy to be leaving London and the UK, and to be performing my very first season in a strange place like Jersey. Turns out Jersey wasn't strange at all, it was a wonderful place – and I fell in love with it straight away. I also fell in love. But that my friends, is another story!

Jersey seemed like a million miles away from the grimy, crazy world of south-east London. It's a small island, only nine by five miles, and I loved it. I loved the beautiful beaches and the painted houses, the restaurants and the shops. The people were so different too – far more polite and refined than I was used to meeting! But then, as you probably know, Jersey is an island built on money. Most people there had good jobs, good manners and were well-heeled, as it were. Well, so it seemed to me.

Anyway my contract was in a production show at a leisure and sports centre called Fort Regent. And there I am, doing my 10-minute nightly act – which was going down pretty well I may add. I had bugger all to do all day, I'm doing what I love by night and getting paid for it (though not very much) – so I'm pretty happy. So I'm sat eating a rather delicious sandwich on a bench in the sunshine, when this young, extremely attractive girl (accompanied by a friend) comes up to me wearing a badminton skirt, racquet in hand. She stands tapping the racquet slowly against her leg. Well, it just couldn't really get any better, could it?! Until she spoke! She proceeds to tell me, all flashing brown eyes and flicking her blonde hair, that she knows exactly how my best tricks are done!! What the ...!? One minute I'm sat minding my own business eating the bloody nice sandwich, next minute I'm being told she knows all about the workings of my magic. Do you want to hear this girl's version of events? Do you?

Well here it is ...

'I recognised Dean from the club, so I decided to go over and tell him that I knew the secrets of some of his stage tricks. He looked utterly annoyed with me, stopped eating his sandwich, and put it down very firmly on the bench. He then proceeded to tell me in no uncertain terms that I knew nothing of the sort! 'So what do you think you know?' he demanded! He then gave me this huge, long story that went on forever and in every direction about magic. 'Is there anything else you want to know?' he prac-

tically yelled, before picking up his sandwich in a very deliberate manner as if to say, 'This conversation is now OVER.''

'That's enough of that,' I thought, 'who does she think she is?!' She'd ruined my day. Turned out she had found a place to view my act from behind the stage, which is how she discovered the secret of this one particular trick – which is *not good* for a magician. I was not happy. Anyway, a few days later, I saw her again. Only this time she's all dressed up in high heels and a short skirt – and ignoring me. I was the famous (!) young magician performing in Jersey – but who was she? Suddenly of course, I was interested. And the chase began. She doesn't remember it like this though!

'I was walking with my mum along the street having just finished work; I was working in a bank then. I was wearing heels, but a smart three-piece suit, not a short skirt! Suddenly I was thrown to the floor. My mum thought I was being mugged – but it was Dean. He had seen me and made a dive for me, tripping me over. He insisted I go to his next show. Well after recovering myself from off the ground, I said I would think about it – knowing all along that I would go, of course.'

She could have been desperate to see me, but if she was she didn't show it. Typical girl. Acting all distant in front of her mum. But looking back, I don't think my act was *that* good, even if I thought so at the time. But my ego was colossal – that I am certain of! But we did meet up, giving me just enough time to cast a magic spell on her! Haha! I tell her she can come round to my luxury abode (the skanky room in a house I was sharing). Well, I don't know what came over me, I like playing little practical jokes for some reason. So I did this thing ...

'Firstly, I did meet up with Dean in the club. He showed me this 'party trick' with a can of Coke. I had no way of knowing what a practical joker he was. He made me balance this can of Coke on my head. Well, guess what happened next – the Coke ended up all over me and this special sweater that my mum had lovingly knitted for me. (I had to hide it and never did tell her what happened to it.) He invited me round to his 'apartment' – and I

imagined this smart little place – it was nothing of the sort! So the next day I went around to see him. I stayed for a while and then said I had to leave because I had a 'sensible job' to go to. Well Dean thought he'd surprise me with another one of his little jokes ... and proceeded to tip a huge bucket of water over me from the upstairs window as I left. I went back to work with my suit dripping wet and squelching shoes – to an office of people who wanted to know what happened to me on such a lovely, hot summer's day! It was a wool suit too, and the water carried on pouring out of it for the whole of the rest of the afternoon. Why on earth did I go back for more? I must have been a sucker for punishment!'

In truth she was a sucker for punishment – but thankfully she didn't realise this at the time!

Chapter 9

AND SO IT was that my truly magical summer season in Jersey came to an end. Sue, for that was her name, this cheeky, pretty girl with the badminton racquet and I had become inseparable. We just knew that we had to be together. From here in though I will call her Claudine – all will become clear why – just trust me on this! So, *Claudine* was just 18 years old, and I was only 24 (not that old!) – but I wasn't that worldly when it came to girls. I'd been too busy practising my thimble routine than getting off with birds. It's the truth, and if I'm honest, I was still concerned about Claudine getting too serious with me. I had no idea where I was going, or what I would do when I returned to the UK. I never imagined for one minute that I would fall in love. I just knew that I didn't want to be apart from Claudine. So when all the great laughs and late nights and days on the beach together came to an end, and I went back to the London grime, we would talk for hours on the phone about her leaving the island. This caused terrible anguish for Claudine's parents, who had very mixed feelings about her leaving Jersey – but in all honesty – they had very mixed feelings about me too. Not that I understood any of this at the time. Now though, I can see that the thought of having their only daughter go to live in rough old London, with no money or prospects would be such a worry for them. They hardly knew me – they must have wondered whether I could look after her. Understandably, Claudine's mother Madeline was particularly upset that her 'baby', the last sibling in the nest so to speak, was leaving. Especially as they were so close and had a wonderful mother/daughter bond.

But we didn't stop talking about it or dreaming about it (remember – 'you gotta dream ... '). So a few months later

Claudine packed in her job, said goodbye to her friends and her family and joined me in London. It was a massive culture shock for her. I was living in Lewisham – not even a little bit like Jersey – crap basically! Well, the bit where I was living was anyway! Fortunately I had some one-night shows booked for my solo act, which at least kept us in rented accommodation for a while. I met many 'characters' here too – including the world renowned bare-knuckle fighter, Lenny McLean, known just as 'The Guv'nor.' I met Lenny at a gym in Catford, he was always really friendly towards me and even helped me out a few times. On one occasion he was working the doors of this big night club – there was always a bit of aggro with the guys hassling Claudine or my props getting messed with, so I would ask Lenny to keep an eye out. It usually only ever needed a quick word from him and things where sorted – but sometimes people would push their luck – not a good idea with Lenny!

The problem with being an entertainer is that you have all these long, enforced periods with no work – so you find yourself having to duck and dive, having to somehow survive in between doing ordinary jobs around London. In these frustrating periods of idleness I was working on ways to include Claudine in my act. I kept thinking about those guys yelling – 'You gotta have a bird, mate, if you're gonna do magic ...' Maybe they were right, but it had to be the *right* bird, right? Claudine had no background whatsoever in show business, had obviously never been to stage school and she wasn't a dancer. She was, however, keen to be part of the act. I ribbed her that the less she wore the more interesting it would be (which isn't strictly true, but you get my drift). She always pulled a face at this! There was so much for her to learn, but she also had to try and find out who *she* was, if that makes sense. It takes a colossal amount of confidence to walk out onto a stage, you have no idea – and to do it for the first time – I'll let Claudine explain how she felt ...

'Leaving Jersey and knowing I had no friends or family in the UK made me feel so vulnerable. Life was much, much

tougher in London. The commuting that is necessary to work in London was worse than I thought it would be – and as for being Dean's assistant – I was trying my best but I was completely and totally out of my comfort zone. Dean was already accomplished and professional, he had been on the stage since he was young and I knew I had to compliment him, but I definitely wasn't ready for the harshness and criticism that went with it. Finally, after rehearsing my part in one of his acts, I got together the courage to join him on stage. After, I think, only my second performance – a man in the audience told me after the show that I looked fat, and that I had huge thighs! I admit I was perhaps a bit 'plump' to be a sexy assistant, but I was really shocked and went to find Dean to tell him. I expected some comfort and for him to say, 'Just ignore the idiot,' but instead he said 'Perhaps he's right!' Thanks Dean! I knew I needed to trim up a bit though and after this I started dieting, but without success. Everything was just so bloody tough. It was exciting too though. Dean was so passionate about his magic, and although we had no idea where we were going, we were both excited about the future. We knew that we wanted to work as a magic duo, and in all truth, we were just really happy to be together.

Then Dean was asked to do an audition for a brand new talent show called New Faces. It was 1986. It was to be filmed live at The Hippodrome in Birmingham. Some months later Dean's agent received a call from the producers to say that he was one of the successful ones (there were over 3000 applicants), and that he would appear live on this new TV show very soon. Unlike shows now – where literally anybody can audition doing practically anything, the auditions for New Faces only involved proven talented acts, many of whom had their own agents, so it was a real honour to be selected. I had only appeared on stage a few times at this point and didn't want to assist Dean for this show – no way was I going on stage live on TV in front of millions of people! But I did go with him to the filming. Dean did really well, and received great comments from the all three of the judges – comedian Bernard Manning, radio presenter Kid Jenson and the most hated of all of the judges – the columnist Nina Myskow. She was always introduced as 'The Wicked Witch of Wapping' – but even she was complimentary about Dean. We were both really happy with how it all went.

This show was a bit of a turning point and a few offers started to come in. We also, at this time, arranged to have our very first publicity photo done together. We had these printed and sent them out to hundreds of agents in the UK and abroad. Slowly Dean and I worked on different ways that I could be part of the act, and each time we performed together I gained more confidence. I still desperately wanted to get myself in better shape though – but wasn't succeeding – probably not helped by the fact that we both loved to go out and hit the clubs – drinking loads and eating loads! I think it's fair to say that I perhaps wasn't the most disciplined and dedicated magician's assistant!

My parents did come over to see us perform in London but they found it all a bit intimidating I think. I can't blame them really. Catford and Croydon and some other rough old places we stayed in were a bit of an eye opener for them, and then there was the performance side of things. They didn't understand about me developing into a sexy assistant. However, they could never do enough for us both and would take us out for posh meals and bring Dean bottles of whisky over from Jersey. So thinking about this now – it's probably their fault that he drinks too much of the stuff! Although he admits that it was his own father who got him started on it! But just in case you was wondering – he actually isn't an alcoholic!

So following our publicity campaign, we started to get bookings for more shows, which was fantastic. We even had a booking for several months for a club in Spain – which we were really happy about – as you can imagine! Turns out the club owner was seriously dodgy and refused to pay us, leaving us high and dry after a few weeks and with Dean narrowly avoiding being arrested. Less said about that one the better! The following year, however, we secured what we thought was going to be our best contract to date. Dean was over the moon as he started to tell me all about it … and I was starting to get really excited too. And then he told me where it was. It was in Syria.'

Our very first photo together – taken in 1986

Chapter 10

MY JAW DROPPED; 'Syria?' I asked. 'Yes,' said Dean,' Syria.' There was no time to think about the possible implications of that, other than obviously agreeing to dress appropriately in this Muslim country, because just a few days later we were on a plane to France. Landing at Charles de Gaulle Airport, we found ourselves joining a whole troupe of French dancers and we all boarded a flight to Damascus. It was on the flight to Damascus that I got a chance to see the publicity brochure for the show. My eyes nearly popped out of my head. Never mind being advised to 'dress appropriately!' This was a 'full nudity show.' 'Yeah, so what?' Dean answered without looking up when, completely shocked, I showed him the brochure! Did he know about this? How on earth were we going to share a dressing room with 30 naked dancers? How would I cope – I was still so insecure about being 'plump?' And being a Muslim country – where women kept themselves covered at all times – would I even be safe? He refused to be drawn on the subject. My heart was pounding as we came into land.

We were taken immediately to a five-star hotel, called The Cham Palace Hotel. Apart from the entertainers, there were few women to be seen. Leaving the hotel was so frightening because large groups of men would gather around me and look me up and down – and not because I was a star or a celebrity – but purely because I was a woman out in public without a hijab or veil. It felt very dangerous to me.

The first time we did the show at the hotel I was so scared, stripping off in front of all the slim dancers, but I soon learned that Arab men prefer plumper women because they assume you are rich – presumably because you can afford to eat loads of food! I felt okay after that and Dean PROMISED me that he wasn't looking at all the naked dancers – although years later he confessed to me that of course he looked at the girls, but as he always says 'No harm in looking!'

The show was going okay and I stopped worrying, but then after about a week I got very ill and started vomiting. I had serious food poisoning and was unable to keep fluids down, let alone eat. Doctors were called in every day to give me painful injections, it was horrible. In the UK I would have been admitted to hospital, but I most certainly didn't want to go to hospital in Syria, I might never get out! So I just coped as best I could.

After about eight days I was finally able to eat and walk again, I was very weak but I had to get back to the show. Dean and I were going over a few things in our room and needed me to check something or other with reception. The hotel was a big, American-style building with huge lobbies on each floor and extra-large, double-sized lifts. I waited for the lift and as the wide, double doors opened I stepped inside. Just a second before they closed, a large man flew through the gap – I remember thinking 'Where did he come from?' – I hadn't seen him in the lobby? As soon as the doors closed he got hold of me by the collar and threw me to the other side of the lift. It was so unexpected and he threw me with such force that I didn't have time to react, I just hit the corner. He then grabbed hold of me again, pressing himself into me really hard – I tried to thump him but he had hold of me so tightly and I was so weak that it had no effect at all. He threw me again – back into the other corner so hard that I thought he was going to kill me. He then pressed himself up against me again, shoving his hands under my clothes and grabbing all over my body. I was barely able to move and knew exactly what he was going to do next when I realised I could just reach the lift buttons. I punched every single one of them and suddenly the lift stopped and the doors opened. I let out the loudest scream I could muster and the man took his hands out of my clothes, looked at me like I was a piece of dirt and calmly walked off. No-one came to my rescue – it was just another large, empty lobby. I went straight back up to Dean, I was shaking so hard and could hardly speak. He could see that I was totally traumatised and after I'd told him what happened he yelled 'Right, that's it, I'm going to find him!' I pleaded with him not to go, this man was vicious and I was scared for Dean. I was shaken up but I was not hurt, but Dean wouldn't have it. He stormed off out of the room, fists clenched, determined to find him. Funny thing was, he'd been shaving when I ran back into the room to tell him what had happened, and he hadn't washed the shaving foam off his face – so he ran down the corridor looking like a very angry Father Christmas!

I followed him and we went down to the second floor. I thought this man would have disappeared after what he did to me, but when the lift doors opened I couldn't believe it – there he was – standing in the foyer. I was still shaking and now I was frightened that Dean would get hurt. 'Is that him?' Dean asked and I just nodded. That was when I saw a different side to Dean, he lunged straight for him and punched him hard in the head, he was furious and my God, it showed. I couldn't watch, I was terrified that he was going to get seriously hurt. I turned away and covered my face, listening to all the wallops and punches going on. It went quiet for a moment and I heard Dean say, 'Shall I kill him, or shall I just hit him once more?' It's funny the things you remember at times like this, but I literally remember thinking 'You'd better not kill him, as this is Syria after all.' So I just peeped around and said 'Okay. Once more.' Dean had this man by the throat, he was a big man, much taller than Dean – but he gave him one final whack, really hard in the head again – and boy, that felt good, that one felt like it was from me! He then stepped away, his fists still clenched and the man staggered off. We never saw him again.

After that I rarely left Dean's side, feeling safer if I was right next to him – or at least in the same room. But I was in for another frightening experience, as if what had happened wasn't bad enough. On New Year's Eve all the entertainers and dancers were invited to an after-show party and dinner. The dancers hadn't been given a glass of wine, so I offered to ask around to see if I could find some for them. I asked a few people and somebody advised me to go to the manager's office in the restaurant. It was only in the adjoining room but no sooner had I entered the manager's room another man came in behind me and locked the door, taking the key out of the lock! I could hear all the people talking and laughing close by, but now here I was in a locked room with two men. This time I flipped, screaming that my husband would be looking for me in two minutes (I obviously didn't know that for sure – but I sure wanted it to be true). I seriously shouted for all I was worth, and eventually they unlocked the door and let me go. Once again I was frightened and shaking all over. What was it with this place?

When it came to be paid, they gave us our salary in local currency – which when converted in UK sterling turned out to be a lot less than we had expected. All the French dancers were in tears, as they depended on their solo income even more than us. Personally I didn't care. I just couldn't wait to leave.

We left, homeward bound at last. Back in the UK we agreed – it wasn't the best contract we'd had, but hoped the next one would be better.'

Chapter 11

Talking of Claudine, I must tell you how she became my wife. Actually, I might let Claudine tell you that one – you women are so much better at that stuff than us!

'Dean didn't so much as propose, as far as he was concerned it was just a foregone conclusion that we were going to be getting married – and soon! So much for him supposedly getting worried that I was getting too clingy! On the other hand – that's the way I saw it too. As Dean says, 'we just knew we needed to be together.' We had very little money at this time in our lives, so we settled for a small ceremony in Croydon with just a few friends and family. I found a lovely wedding dress and we did hire a brilliant photographer who dressed as Charlie Chaplin for the day – and he captured some wonderful photos. One crazy thing though; we bought our matching wedding rings from Hatton Garden and we were really proud of them. But just before the wedding, we had one of them (not both of them?) stolen from our flat and there was a real panic to get another one made. After the service at the church we went back to our little flat in Croydon where we laid on lots of champagne and nibbles and drank a bit too much! Dean had arranged a posh white Mercedes to whisk us off for a couple of nights in Eastbourne – but instead a black Mercedes arrived with no ribbons on it! Dean was bloody furious and insisted the driver drop us off at the chauffeur's office to have it out with them – but by then I think we were both too pissed to care!

As for Eastbourne, I wouldn't call it a luxury hotel, but there were promises of a four-poster bed. We did get the four-poster but the thing that annoyed Dean the most was that the kitchen door was literally right next to our door – and the staff were up early setting up for breakfast the very next morning and their door kept banging every single time they entered or left the kitchen! When Dean explained to reception why he was unhappy and what the problem was – they just looked at him like 'What's the problem, man?' I just remember hearing a lot of swearing (I got used to this) as Dean proceeded to demonstrate the noise we were hearing at 5am. He stood and slammed our door three or four times really hard and then asked them how they felt about it. I think they got the message because they moved us instantly! Lastly, and this might sound really stupid, but the main thing I remember about Eastbourne – apart from loads of really old people walking around with Zimmer frames – was breakfast. When we went to the restaurant area it was dead quiet – you know when you can hear even a whisper – there were all these old people sat at the tables literally not speaking to each other. Dean was trying to open one of those individually wrapped butter portions – you know the ones I mean? Now these really get on his nerves because they always give them to you when they are totally frozen solid – do they deliberately keep them in the freezer over-night?? So he tries to be patient – he waits for it to melt a bit and then decides to squeeze the wrapper a little to help the butter to come out – but he squeezes too hard and the butter goes flying into the air and lands on this old guy's shoulder. He has a proper smart jacket on too, and well, all I can say is he's not impressed to end up with butter on it at breakfast. I collapse into giggles, which I find hard to control, and this sets us both off laughing hysterically!'

So now officially man and wife, we resumed our usual routine of making calls to entertainment agents and sending out another new set of publicity brochures – honestly, the money we've spent putting together this promotional material over the years has run into many thousands of pounds – but it had to be done. Our act was a continually evolving thing and we were constantly having to update the information and photographs we sent out, to best represent what we were doing at any given time.

Incidentally, we ought to have a formal bit in here somewhere about birth, dates and names. Here seems as good a place as any! I was born in 1961 and given the name Dean Metcalfe. After winning The Young Magician of the Year I adopted the name Deano for a short time, if you remember, but I soon dropped this. I then went by the stage name of Carl Dean, which I liked – it had a certain ring to it. And then I met Claudine, but perhaps I should say Susan Marie. Sue hated being called Sue – she says it has too much of a girl-next-door feel to it. So when she joined me in London and then became part of my magic, we chose 'Claudine' as her stage name. So we became 'Carl Dean and Claudine.' But people being the sort of people that they are sometimes – they had a problem with this. They said it was a bit of a tongue-twister! And then there were those who would ask, 'So if you're Carl Dean and she's Claudine and you're now married, does that mean Claudine is now called Claudine Dean?' Honestly, this is how it would go. So around this time, with working so many different clubs etc, we gave this name thing some thought. In fact we gave it quite a lot of thought – and we decided to change our names to simply 'The Deans of Magic' – hence the need for more publicity material! Just thought I'd bung that in. Not too confusing for you I hope!?

So we're sat having a cup of tea at home when we get a call from an agent in Luxembourg – he makes us an offer of a contract in Belgium. It couldn't have come at a better time, we had not been working much since Syria and needed money fast. It was slightly closer to home too! I asked her what sort of venue we would be working at – and she told me it was an eight-week contract at one of the finest night clubs in Europe – I didn't hear much else, I don't even think I waited to hear the fee! I just accepted the contract and we started to pack once again. This was the break we needed and the agent said the contract may even be extended. We were happy.

Since returning from Syria I noticed that Claudine had lost her 'plump' look, as she called it. She was working out with steely determination, inspired by the professional dancers we had worked with out there. Everyone was saying how great she looked and she was on the lookout for something sensational and skimpy to wear – how things change – gone were the frowns and sighs from before! And boy oh boy! Did we find that sensational outfit! But I'll tell you about that later. So here we are again, all packed up and ready to go and work (and earn some money!) at this top European club. We are excited about journeying to Belgium and the ideas we have for our show.

We travelled from London to Brussels via the Dover ferry (awkward seeing as we were carrying all of our props with us!) – and needed a taxi urgently. The weather was atrocious – and I mean *really* atrocious – like all the rain in the world decided to fall in one gigantic monsoon over Brussels all in one go! We struggled from taxi to taxi trying to get one of them to take us to the club, but the drivers simply refused to take us, saying that we had too much luggage with us. In the end we persuaded one driver who named his price – which turned out to be ten times the going rate, as we later discovered – and collapsed into the cab, soaking wet but relieved to be on our way. We gave the driver the address and he shot us a look, started the car and drove on checking us out in the mirror. We arrived at the street ... that's when we noticed all the red lights. This time we shot each other a look. Our 'top European club' was in the seediest looking street I'd ever clapped eyes on – lined with large posters of topless women! It was like being in London's Soho in the bleeding sixties! Not exactly the classy establishment we had in mind!

We again struggled from the taxi, heaving all the gear out in the horrendous pouring rain and dumping it in the club's reception area. We were greeted by Madame Corrine, who had this habit of rolling her eyes to heaven, before yelling the answer to every question we asked her. Where were we, for Lord's sake? We battled on, thinking – just a few more minutes and we can get all the kit to our room, have a hot shower and then head out for some food – we hadn't eaten all day and were starving. It was then that I noticed that Claudine's make-up case was missing. This was no ordinary make-up case – it was a big aluminium professional case full of very expensive professional stage make-up. I asked our dear Madame Corrine if she had seen it. 'You think I've stolen your case – you English bastard? Do you? You think I've stolen your case?' she shouted. But not before rolling her eyes so far they nearly flew out of the top of her head! What a start!

We eventually booked in and the lovely Madame Corrine took us up to our accommodation. It can only be described as disgusting. The bed was a filthy mattress on the floor. The toilet was in the middle of the room – next to the bed. There were no curtains, the wallpaper was hanging off the damp walls and there was a horrendous, dirty smell in the air – like boiled rabbit heads or bones – whatever that smells like! Just trust me on this – it was an evil smell. By now we were cold, wet, hungry, worried about the make-up case *and* appalled at the state of our room. We just couldn't get our minds off the missing case though and decided to walk back to the station, to save money, to see if we could find it. We didn't even have the will to change our wet clothes, so we headed out back into the torrential rain in the clothes we were wearing – which were smart, city clothes really. We always dressed smartly when we travelled and today was no different. Poor Claudine though, she was wearing a black pencil skirt and black high heels, which were now as good as ruined.

We made our way to the station, by now at the end of our endurance. We looked for the taxi we had taken, to see if it had returned. We walked around the station, but couldn't see him anywhere. Claudine was holding onto my hand, we were miserable and so hungry – could things get much worse? They did. As we walked through the station Claudine slipped on what can only be described as custard or banana milkshake or some other yellow substance that had been spilled on the marble floor. Her feet flew up in the air and she crashed down into the yellow stuff which splattered all up her legs and back and into her hair. If I hadn't have been holding her hand she could have been seriously hurt – but I managed to slow her fall. It was then that we decided to give up and go back to the club and try to get Claudine cleaned up. We couldn't see the taxi anywhere. But as we turned the corner we saw him parked outside the club – he'd found the case and driven back with it – fantastic news! Suddenly he was the best taxi driver in the world! Until he had the gall to ask for the same fare again for bringing the case back! Now he wasn't the best taxi driver in the world. We refused to pay and he threatened us with the mafia. *The mafia*! And if things could have got any worse – Madame Corrine heard the shouting and came out to join in. Bloody hell. She got well stuck in and needless to say, the taxi driver did not win this one. Between the three of us we convinced him that we *were not paying!* We couldn't have been more exhausted by now, but were so relieved to have got the case back.

We staggered up to our room, almost oblivious to the shit state of it. But our next problem was getting Claudine cleaned up in such a disgusting hovel and getting some food. We decided that Claudine would stay behind and I should take a taxi and go and get us a burger, I'd seen a McDonald's near the station – isn't there a bloody McDonald's in every bloody town and city across the whole bloody world?! But on this occasion it seemed like a Michelin star restaurant. So once again I headed out onto the rain-soaked streets, wondering if my grandfather had anything to do with this chaos. I found a taxi and asked the driver to wait while I grabbed some burgers. He did. I climbed back in – ordeal nearly over – two big bags of McDonald's on my lap. All was good until the driver slammed the brakes on to avoid a truck and the bags of McDonald's became suddenly airborne, turned upside down mid-flight and landed all over the floor of the cab. Do you know what? I didn't give a shit then. I just scooped all the food back into the bags, paid the driver and headed back to our room. Claudine mentioned the bits of fluff and hair on the burgers, but was too hungry to care.

Our top class European club turned out to be a hostess club; the audience weren't remotely interested in our magic – they had their minds on other things – particularly what was happening in the corner to the left of the stage where ladies did unmentionable things to gentlemen who quaffed champagne before, during and after the event!

In the day, sat in our hideous room with no TV, no radio, no English newspapers and the toilet in the middle, we were curious to find out what was causing this incessant and loud rapping noise. We looked out of the filthy window down into the street and watched as men on the other side of the road – also curious about this very loud rapping noise – would turn and try to identify the source of the racket. It was then that they would take a slow glance around, cross over to our side of the street and disappear. We had to go and investigate and were astonished to find a woman with *enormous* breasts in the window! We found out that she spent her day on all fours, dressed in a bikini, rapping loudly on the window with a coin! When she got the attention of the chap on the other side of the street, she would beckon him over whilst pressing the colossal breasts against the window – I'm guessing to make them look *bigger* – if that was even possible, and let him in. So our entertainment in the day was watching the guy's reactions and if they went in – timing how long they were in there! Which was on average about three or four minutes!! Unbelievable!! What was that all about?!

We managed just three weeks of that contract. It was a hell hole. How unfortunate can two performers get? Years later though, we discovered that some pretty established artists performed in that club – just shows you how desperate times can get when you're in the entertainment industry. We did find that sensational, skimpy outfit though. We discovered this incredible make-up and costumiers shop in Brussels and it was here that we found the costume that Claudine had had the vision about. It was stunning, and she looked stunning in it. It was always a joke wherever she performed in this particular outfit that it could fit in the palm of one closed hand! But as fate would have it – it definitely had something to do with the many bookings that followed in the years to come! Wow!

Chapter 12

ONCE AGAIN WE were back in the UK, exhausted but relieved to be away from the shit hole in Belgium. One of Europe's top clubs, my arse! You've got to laugh really. And Madame Corrine – what a scary woman! All that eye-rolling and yelling – mad! And the woman with the huge breasts in the window! Despite all the crazy stuff, we still laugh when we remember those times.

I remember when Claudine got chicken pox, which is a lot more serious when you're an adult. Great time to nearly meet Max Clifford! She was in bed for several weeks in a lot of pain, with a high fever, and covered with those awful dark blisters that you get with chicken pox. And I mean, *absolutely covered*. Finally she felt well enough to get up and go out for a while. She wanted to find some moisturiser and concealer for her face, which was looking pretty grim! The blisters had all burst, but were all scabby and horrible. So she ventured out in a jacket and hat, with a scarf wrapped around her face and her hood up too. We went down to Bentall's Shopping Centre in Kingston-upon-Thames and into Selfridges to try to find her some creams. We approached the cosmetics counter and of course, there was this immaculate, flawless female assistant waiting to serve us. She looked at Claudine in total horror. We explained about the chicken pox, 'Oh my goodness,' she said, reaching out and actually touching the scabs on Claudine's face, 'I've never had chicken pox – it would be a disaster for me to get something like that in my profession of beauty and make-up, wouldn't it!' And then, as if in a slow-motion sort of movie clip, we watched as she took her fingers away from Claudine's spots and absent-mindedly put them in her mouth …

A bit later on we both laughed our heads off at that – is that cruel?! It's just that Claudine hadn't been out for ages, and certainly hadn't laughed for a very long time – and that was what probably made us laugh more than it should have done! Then the almost-meeting-Max-Clifford-thing happened. Only just the *famous celebrity publicist and PR agent Max Clifford*. I couldn't believe my eyes. He was sat having a quiet drink in the bar of Selfridges and we were sat right next to him. I really, really wanted to talk to him. I mean *really*. But I knew that any conversation would have to include Claudine, who looked like an extra from a horror movie – rather than the UK's sexiest magician's assistant, so I had to leave it. Bugger!

So anyway, despite having only been in Belgium for three weeks, we had enough cash for a deposit on a new abode. We found a place in Croydon – but again we seem to end up in one of the less prosperous areas, as it were! We got pretty good at blagging our way into renting these flats – largely due to fact that we had the cash to pay a few month's rent upfront. There was little chance of us being able to produce the usual references – the cash did the talking thankfully – and we managed to convince the landlords that we had that sort of money coming in as regular income. Nothing could have been further from the truth!

We move into the flat, staying up late at night talking about magic and coming up with ideas for our shows and the music we could use to accompany the acts. We don't play the music loudly, we're not being inconsiderate like that, but we still drive our neighbours mad staying up to the wee hours rehearsing. The wafer-thin partition walls and the creaky floor boards didn't help much either – all those poor buggers who had to get up in the morning for their nine-to-five jobs – they must have hated us. But we were night owls and had so much to organise.

I started to get pretty critical of Claudine, analysing her every move – just the way I was scrutinised. That sounds like I was being horrible, I wasn't – but we both knew we had to get the best out of her. Sexy assistants had to be as sexy as possible – so we worked really hard – making sure she felt confident with what she was doing. One of our late-night ideas turned out to be a huge hit in our performances. We had a dress designed for Claudine with all these invisible poppers. It could be ripped off in one move – to reveal the rather skimpy, sexy number we had bought in Belgium. It wasn't a fancy dress, quite plain really and long to hide Claudine's incredible legs and high heels – but oh boy! The reaction of the audience when we first used that dress! Funnily enough – we got a surprising number of men wanting to know where they could buy such a dress!

I'm also working very hard to get the magic as slick and cool as possible, with the tricks accompanied by the appropriate music. We really liked the sound track of Beverly Hills Cop by Axel F, which was a big hit at this particular time. I want to use lit candles in the act too, as flames always add drama to the tricks. I adapt a trick with a cane – to make it look luminous – we use UV light on stage and I wear white gloves. It is visually stunning to watch – all the audience can see are the white gloves and the cane dancing around in the strange light – it looked so good. But I'm still trying to figure out how to include more flames or lights in our act. Claudine is not short of ideas herself, but the problem is we just haven't got the money or resources to create these ideas. People don't realise, but these props cost a lot of money – particularly when you design and build a prototype that quite often needs several re-builds before it's stage-worthy. But she did have one idea that stuck with me. Remember the floating Sacred Sun Ball? Well Claudine had this idea that we could use a small chandelier in a similar way – getting it to float around a piece of silk in a similar way to the ball. I initially rule it out, but it begins to play on my mind and I keep coming back to it, trying to work out how it could be done.

We also bought a confetti launcher, with a view to making the end of our show more spectacular. Our finale definitely needed work – how were we to know that the confetti launcher most certainly *wouldn't* be the way to do that! But we're dying to try it out. We have a good look at the thing; it's a metal box, about five inches square with a welded tube on the top that's about 12 inches long. You basically unscrew the bottom of the box, place an explosive device called a maroon inside (which has a long wire coming from it that is attached to another plastic box with – guess what – a 9-volt battery inside!), shove the thing full of confetti and hey presto! You're ready to go! The instructions warn you that this device should only be used in a large open space – but we decide to ignore that . . . and set it up on the floor of our little lounge. There is also a warning that the 'bang' the device produces is rather loud – we don't ignore this – and duly inform our neighbours of the impending 'explosion.' Pretty good of us, don't you think?

We go back into our flat, run the wire from the maroon across the floor to just outside the lounge door where we can safely peep round to watch how things proceed. We nip back in to check that the windows are closed – don't want to startle the people out in the street after all – and then duck back down behind the door. I first pull down on the switch of the 'detonator' and then without another thought press down hard on the bright red button. Well, bloody hell, there is this instant, massive explosion that I can only describe as several shot guns all being fired simultaneously and this acrid smell of explosives. Me and Claudine leap up from our hiding place and are greeted by the sight of smoke and confetti flying literally everywhere – even down the holes in the back of the telly!! We go into the room and that's when we realise that both panes of glass in the windows have cracked! I go to the metal launcher to check it and badly burn my hands trying to pick it up – it's red hot! And also stuck to the carpet! *The landlord's new carpet! Shit!* Eventually we get the thing moved, to reveal a dark, black, square burn – no matter – we buy a rug to cover that as it was quite close to the fireplace anyway and looks totally acceptable.

Despite all this malarkey, we're still keen to use it in our closing act and start looking for slighter larger venues than our lounge. Strangely though, health and safety were not as keen as us – perhaps because we made the mistake of telling them about our little test-run! In the end we abandon the thing and if we're totally honest, we were a little bit of afraid of it ourselves after the event in our flat.

Chapter **13**

BY THE MID-EIGHTIES bookings are starting to come in again and the shows are going really well. We are spotted by a well-known agency in the north of England. They want us to perform in The Falklands for our British troops.

By now I've gone through the whole thing of not reading the contract and getting a nasty surprise, or reading the contract and still getting a nasty surprise – so yep, you're right – I didn't bother reading the contract. I suppose I could also have done a bit more research about what to expect out there, but I didn't do that either. All I knew was we were heading out to islands that had been at war and that the audience most certainly would be made up entirely of men. But that didn't bother me either, our show – although not consciously – was definitely turning into something that appealed more and more to men. I was aware of the stronger and stronger reactions Claudine was getting and as far as I was concerned, it would be the perfect opportunity to fully test this new aspect of our show, with the ripping off of Claudine's dress and the great music etc. Little did we know that despite the good bits, this trip would be such a physical test of our endurance.

We flew from RAF Brize Norton in Oxfordshire, an 18-hour flight that included a re-fuel in the Ascension Islands. When we touched down in The Falklands we were seriously jet lagged and ready for the cold but we were completely unprepared for *how* cold it was – it was absolutely and literally bloody freezing. The landscape was very barren; this was going to be no picnic, but we had to give it a chance. We were immediately transported to our accommodation; a portakabin. It was basic, but warm, and a vast improvement on our digs in Belgium I have to say. As you can imagine, the whole thing was run with military precision and within a very short space of time we had been made very welcome, had been invited to eat in the main dining quarters – the food was hot and delicious – and had been introduced to the guys in charge of lighting and PA. These guys immediately got started setting up all the equipment for all the entertainers; a singer, a comedian, dancers and of course, ourselves.

By now you probably appreciate that a magic act like ours requires a lot of delicate props that have to be set up prior to the performance. Lighting and mood are very important factors for creating the right atmosphere too. The settings at 'venues' like this were hardly ideal – generally in the canteen with all the chairs cleared away to make room for the 'stage'; the lighting and sound was pretty awful for magic too – but the guys were so helpful and the soldiers so appreciative that none of this mattered really. They couldn't wait to be entertained by us civvies and the standard of the acts was excellent, everybody did everything they possibly could to give their best and the atmosphere was always fantastic.

I have to tell you about our first night with these troops, it was incredible, absolutely incredible. I walk onto stage with slightly robotic moves to Axel F pumping out the Beverly Hills Cop theme tune, I'm wearing an Italian jacket that is short and tight – like the type with tails, but without the tails if you can visualise that. My hair (I had loads of black hair back then!) is gelled back and I'm wearing these Terminator style sunglasses. In my hand I'm holding an unlit candle. I stand centre stage and I do not move. I remain completely still.

After a few moments Claudine follows wearing the long, quite ordinary dress that we designed and her hair tucked up inside a trilby hat. She is holding a large stick that is on fire, and with a stylish flourish lights my candle. I still have not moved an inch at this point and you can feel the anticipation from the audience. Now I am a small guy, and you can bet some of those big, strong blokes are thinking 'Who does he think he is ... ?' But in an instant my candle goes up in a huge flash of flames, in the same moment that, still wearing the shades, I rip off Claudine's dress, she turns her flames into an evening cane, throws off her hat to reveal her long blonde hair and that sensational next-to-nothing costume we bought in Belgium! The guys erupt! The room is filled with terrific roars and Claudine soaks up the attention – knowing she has finally arrived! What a response.

During the show Claudine walks on and off stage several times – to rapturous applause and stamping and whistling – bringing on or taking away various props. She works the audience, teasing them with sensual gestures to me, all with that now perfected cheekiness. I quickly learn not to try to perform any magic when Claudine is on stage as all eyes are on her, not me! She's bloody stolen the show! But I don't care, I'm a happy boy –and if anything the guys are beginning to appreciate my magic even more now. And I realise in this very moment that the chemistry between Claudine and myself is a magic all of its own, a magic that cannot be engineered, it's just so good. And somewhere along the way we also realise that it doesn't matter so much if people don't remember all the tricks, it's just great that they remember us and like us. We worked in some amazing places as a result of that dress and Claudine's vision about that sexy outfit ... but that is all to come! Maybe Belgium wasn't so bad to us, after all.

Anyway, back to The Falklands. It was tough there, my God it was tough. We were treated so well – all the entertainers were – but the schedule was gruelling. The guys would always stay up drinking until the early hours after a show and we were expected to join them, which, don't get me wrong, was such a laugh – but we had to get up at 5 or 6am every morning to be flown by Chinook to our next venue. Our expensive and indeed delicate props were taken in huge great BVs (bridging vehicles) and sometimes we travelled with them – bouncing around in the back in the freezing cold with the kit bouncing around too – not ideal. I was terrible in these vehicles and am ashamed to say that I often vomited! How embarrassing in front of all the big, hard army boys! Sometimes, there was nowhere for Claudine to change and she had to swap costumes outside in the freezing cold – like minus 30 degrees cold. Her health was starting to suffer and to be honest she was looking too thin now as well, but I'll let Claudine tell you about that.

'It's hard being a female in the limelight. You might say that I'm just whining, but really and truly, it's so hard. Your body is so analysed by everyone; how it looks and how your hair looks. I was never that vain, I liked to look nice and dressed smartly for work when I was living in Jersey – but I was gaining so much attention now that I was becoming paranoid.

I took dieting to another level, slowly starting to skip meals and lying to Dean about food until in the end my body was so thin that I found it hard to lie on my back because the bones were protruding so much. What I (we) didn't realise was that I was demonstrating the typical symptoms of anorexia, and that it was becoming quite serious. But according to everyone else and judging by the response from our audiences – I was looking great – so I just carried on starving myself. Inside though I was deteriorating, getting weaker and weaker. We just didn't see what was happening.'

So physically, for many reasons, we were both struggling. The shows were going great, but all the madness and drinking at night and the freezing cold early starts were making us both exhausted. How do these boys keep up this life? They're certainly a lot tougher than us! They'd be drinking and goofing around all night – having crazy competitions like who could jump the furthest to head-butt the bell on the other side of the bar and who could hang the most beer cans off their willies – and then get up in the morning like they'd had their eight hours beauty sleep! And we were wrecked! Psychologically too, working and living in such tough conditions was taking its toll. We were burning out. But our contract in The Falkland Islands was coming to an end, it would soon be time to pack up again and head this time, to Northern Ireland. As part of our contract though, on the way back from The Falklands we had to stop in the Ascension Islands to perform a few shows there. But we both agreed that a few days in the sun en-route to Ireland was just what we needed.

Claudine and our portakabin accommodation in the Falklands

The lads setting up the PA and lighting in the canteen area – not the glamorous setting that we had been expecting!

Chapter 14

We checked and packed all our gear and said goodbye to everyone. Flying over The Falklands for the last time we looked down at the mountains and the wild landscape with mixed feelings. What an experience that had been. But we were looking forward to a change now and relaxing in the sunshine for a few days.

The Ascension Islands are a tiny cluster of volcanic islands located between Brazil to the West and Africa to the East. They too are quite barren – but at least it's warm! The military still had a presence there and with the usual enthusiasm warmly welcomed us. On the first night we joined them for drinks – probably a mistake – actually, definitely a mistake. Have you ever heard of 'Fluffy Duck?' No, we hadn't either – but that was what these boys, and officers, were drinking. They put a pint glass of Fluffy Duck in front of Claudine and she drank it. What happened next was awful, really horrible. What we didn't realise until the next day was that the walls of the portakabin were so thin that everybody pretty much heard everything that happened that night . . .!

It was already getting quite late and we were both pretty tired so I whispered to Claudine that we should make a move really. 'I can't feel my legs,' she whispered back. 'What do you mean, you can't feel your legs?' I asked. She confirmed that she actually couldn't feel her legs, as in – she had lost all feeling in them. I suddenly realised she was drunk and so with as much dignity as we could muster, I half led, half carried her out of the mess tent into our assigned portakabin. She immediately started throwing up everywhere, crying and crying, and saying 'I'm dying, Dean! I'm going to die!' She was in a terrible state. Obviously I didn't realise at the time that she hadn't been eating and weighed so little that the alcohol had nowhere to go in her body. She just kept vomiting and crying all night and ended up covered in bruises from falling forwards into the bathroom wall and the toilet pan, it was awful.

Finally daylight came, but Claudine was no better, she was utterly drained, dehydrated and so weak. But we had promised the officers that we would accompany them to a beach party. She begged not to go, but there was no way we could avoid the day out, so we climbed into one of the jeeps with the boys and headed down to the beach. The heat was overwhelming compared to the freezing temperatures in The Falkland Islands, and combined with a night spent throwing up and a bumpy ride in a jeep, Claudine was looking pretty rough by the time we arrived. We tried to socialise but in the end she begged me to let her go and lie down in the cool shadow of a rock to sleep. So off she wandered. I said I'd come and check on her in a while.

'I wandered away from the officers and the other guys, relieved at the thought of finally getting out of the heat and perhaps being able to sleep for a short while. Dean wasn't that impressed but I was desperate so he let me go, saying he would come and find me shortly. I was still throwing up – which was hard – trying to sneak off in front of everybody, and it was so hot, so when I reached the shade of the rock I collapsed with exhaustion. I must have fallen asleep immediately. After what seemed like no time at all I was awoken by Dean who was running up the beach towards me, literally covered in blood and shouting . . . 'CLAUDINE!!'

His arm and back were cut wide open and blood was pouring from the wounds. I obviously had no idea what on earth had happened to him – last time I saw him he was talking to the sound and lighting guys. He was trying to explain but was so shocked himself that none of what he said was making any sense. I clambered to my feet and together we got back into one of the jeeps and were driven, very fast (not good!), to the camp's hospital.

Apparently Dean was taking part in some kind of challenge with the PR boys. It involved being the first one to find a certain crab in the water – the winner would receive a gas soldering iron

– sounds nuts, but a gas soldering iron was a very prized bit of kit – and useful for repairing magic props! Dean was standing on the rocks looking down into the water looking for this crab when a huge wave hit him full-on, sending him flying backwards into the rock – which under normal circumstances would really hurt, but volcanic rock is razor sharp and as he tried to clamber to his feet he was hit again, slicing open his back and right arm and feet. The other guys realised immediately that he was in trouble and thankfully one of them had trainers on and was able to get enough grip on the rock to try to pull him from the water. But the South Atlantic has one of the strongest currents in the world and once again Dean was sucked back into the water. He managed to climb out in the slight lull before the next wave and staggered onto the beach. He was in a really bad state.

He was taken straight to the army surgeon who took one look at Dean's wounds and announced that he would have to inject anaesthetic and antiseptic straight into them. Dean seemed really calm under the circumstances (but I think he was quite probably in shock plus I think he needed to be all tough in front of these big military guys!). But I on the other hand really needed to throw up again – and I was told in no uncertain terms that if I was going to be sick then would I please do so outside! I fled from the room wondering again what on earth we were doing wrong to attract so much disaster? Why was all this stuff happening?

Dean was stitched up, which took ages and then his wounds were dressed. I imagined that we may have to cancel our act that night – but the show must go on as they say. But we were both in a bad way. Dean managed to get his costume on over his dressings, but he was in a lot of pain, and blood still kept dripping down the back of his hand which he had to wipe away when he got the chance to hide what he was doing. I still hadn't been able to eat and felt so ill. But the applause made it kind of all worthwhile!

By the way, Fluffy Duck, in case you were wondering, comprises of the combination of any of the following; Advocaat, white rum, gin, Cointreau, double cream or orange juice and perhaps a splash of soda. It is 85% alcohol and 15% cream or otherwise. Is it any wonder I got so sick? The army don't drink these cocktails in polite-sized cocktail glasses remember, with regular measures – they drink them in pint glasses! Those boys have the constitutions of bloody oxen – I do not! I still shudder when I remember that drink and that night.

What we also found out when we left the Ascension Islands was the horror that are Trigger fish – fish that are attracted to blood and can, like sharks, sense it from like a zillion sea miles away. Wouldn't that have been a suitable finale for Dean after having been ripped open by volcanic rock – drowning in the South Atlantic whilst being eaten by blood-sucking Trigger fish! Nice!

It wasn't long before we were on our way again, this time to extremely volatile Northern Ireland. I wasn't looking forward to this at all and despite the Fluffy Duck nightmare, really loved the Ascension Islands. But work is work and soon we were taking to the skies again, bound for God knows what.'

Chapter 15

So, Northern Ireland in 1988/89. We were there as part of the CSE (Combined Services Entertainments) for the British Forces. The tension and violence between the Loyalists and the IRA had again intensified. We will never forget it. It made Syria look like a holiday camp and The Falklands seem downright safe. We'd got used to travelling in Chinooks or BVs – but armoured vehicles surrounded by fully-armed military with mortars flying overhead – that's something else entirely.

The shows still took place in canteens and once again were hugely well received, but my God, the stress was bad. Every single bang had everybody looking around nervously, it was a bloody nightmare. Hideous stories kept filtering back to us of shootings and stuff and we were both getting pretty tense. And I was getting tired too, if I'm honest, of trying to perform magic in such difficult circumstances and despite the best efforts of the crew around us – coping with the really annoying thrown-together sets. One particular night I was getting really agitated trying to prepare for a trick behind this make-shift curtain that kept falling down. In the end I totally lost my patience with it and slammed my fist down on the table as hard as I possibly could. It was kind of funny what happened next, but not ... a comedian, a chap quite a bit older than ourselves, screamed and threw himself onto the floor – convinced that we had been bombed. Such was the state of all of our nerves. The Falklands were a test on us physically – but psychologically, this was taking us way beyond what we imagined we could endure. We questioned how the people of Northern Ireland had coped living like this for all these years.

Soon enough though, we were on our way back home again. Back to our flat with the burn hole under the rug and whatever would happen next in our glamorous (!) lives as entertainers ...

Chapter 16

We immediately set to preparing for one of the most important annual events on the magic calendar: Ron MacMillan's International Gala at The Empire Rooms in Tottenham Court Road in London. He had been putting on these magic conventions for many years and he would invite the very best of magical talent from across Europe. Ron, incidentally, was also a top international award winning manipulator, like me. His act consisted of the magical appearance of coins and billiard balls. Ron's events were hugely successful and attracted a very large audience of magicians from the UK and abroad. There were lectures and performances all day, concluding with the main gala in the evening – and Claudine and I had been invited to part of that.

We were still working on using more light in our performance and I was trying to work out how to use Claudine's idea of the small, floating chandelier. But I still couldn't seem to come up with a solution. I did have an idea of using a large and beautiful chandelier at the end of our act and immediately started working with an engineering company who agreed to try to build it. We literally worked day and night on the thing as I really wanted to use it to close our act at Ron's magic gala. We did get a chance to test it at The King's Theatre in Glasgow and iron out a few flaws; the chandelier wasn't looking as fully-lit as I wanted it to be – it needed a lot more crystal to produce the required effect. But we still used it for Ron's event, with a pleasing result.

The Empire Rooms is the not the easiest venue to perform in. It's pretty stifling in there, what with all the lights and being packed out with over a thousand magicians, but the energy in the room was electric. A number of acts had performed and been hugely well-received. And then it was our turn. We opened our act precisely as we had done in The Falklands and all hell broke loose;

the response was utterly deafening. Strangely we hadn't expected this reaction from an audience of magicians, but they absolutely loved it and that's all that mattered. Afterwards some of them did venture to say that they weren't looking at me *at all* – that all the focus was now on Claudine – and perhaps that wasn't the best way to present the act! Are you kidding?! All I knew was we were getting the best responses ever to our performances and that that was definitely the way I wanted to present our act in the future. Here is what one well-known magic critic and TV Times columnist said of that night ...

'Two days out of hospital after an eye operation, with a doctor's warning to take it easy, avoid too much excitement and the eyes from disturbances, there I was at the ringside again. Charing Cross Hospital forgot to warn me against little Miss Direction in Carl Dean's act! In fact because of my temporary disability, and need for relief from the tempestuous Miss Direction, I am one of the few who can tell you about Carl Dean's magic.

So, the opening act was Carl Dean. Come on fellas, be honest, even though you got a few nudges from the wife or girlfriend, you never saw Carl did you? He wore dark glasses at the start – well, maybe he's seen it all before. His wife, and assistant, the tantalising Claudine came on wearing a cloak. After Carl vanished a candle she took it off. Wow! Misdirection at its ultimate level!! I'll wager Carl could have produced an elephant without too much trouble as long as Claudine was on stage. I have followed Carl's career since he was runaway prize-winner Dean Metcalfe, offering advice along the way. In the early days his magic was faultless, performed with impish style. Over the years he stripped out the leaden bits, sometimes, but wisely, at the expenses of the ultra clever moves which are not commercial anyway, and now he's smooth as silk. He was always a whisker from the big league, now he's there, and is in that enviable position of being able to work anywhere, and he does. No offence to Claudine of course (eye therapy you know) but I did see the act. Apart from the vanish of lit candles he did a little of his brilliant thimble routine and a three ring routine which is better than most. He dons his cloak and produces a giant candelabra, all shining and bright, just like his act.' Alan Kennaugh.

There is a lot of emphasis on Claudine now and she is loving the attention, wanting to get better and better. But what I didn't see was that it was making her ill and she was losing more and more weight. I noticed that she wouldn't eat very much – if at all – and when we made a trip over to Jersey to see her folks they were really shocked at how thin she was looking. In that sense they really brought it home to me as well and we all got together, knowing we would have to confront her with our concerns. This didn't go down well. She denied there was anything wrong – but was still refusing to eat very much. Eventually we found a lady who specialised in eating disorders and we discovered that Claudine had a severe case of anorexia. This woman turned out to be a real saviour. Through meetings and long talks with Claudine, without me being present, she was able to help Claudine back to health. But it was a long, long battle and all along she bravely continued with the shows. Thankfully, many years later I can now say that she has fully recovered and is happy on occasion to eat more than me! And that's saying something!

A couple of weeks after Ron's Gala we got a call from an agent called Chris Ferguson. He spoke to us about the possibility of supporting various celebrities at a couple of major cabaret clubs in the South of England. We wanted to know more, of course, and before long found ourselves hugely involved in these fantastic events and meeting some great people …

Me in my shades. Looking cool don't you think? However, it wasn't me they were looking at, it was Claudine and that famous skimpy costume that had us in big demand in the night clubs in the 80s

Chapter 17

Our first booking was at a wonderful venue; Blazer's in Windsor. It had a fantastic, full-sized stage, live band and brilliant lighting. I believe it held around a thousand people and was nearly always packed out. These were the days, when people wanted to be properly entertained and even loved the dead basic food that normally arrived in baskets that was included with the ticket price. There was always a great buzz of excitement in this place. We supported countless celebrities here and at other similar venues. One night I can remember walking through the audience and hearing some bloke shout, 'Who's supporting Billy Connolly tonight?' And someone shouted back, 'Oh, some bloody magician!' I just laughed to myself because I knew exactly what this 'bloody magician' had in store for them – and it was certainly not what they were expecting! Our act went down a real storm at these venues.

There was one problem with Blazer's though – I still hadn't passed my driving test – and the obligatory encore (four nights a week) meant that we missed the last train home by just ten minutes. So we would often have to sleep on the, thankfully, big, comfy sofas in the dressing room – which was slightly awkward when the cleaner arrived at 6am every day! I did eventually pass my driving test – which made things a lot easier. We worked with some amazing (and mad) people at this time; Billy Connolly, Hale and Pace, Grace Kennedy, Michael Barrymore and Freddie Star to name but a few. We loved working with Billy though, he was so down to earth and would just wander into our dressing room, plonk himself down in one of the sofas and chat. He loved to see a few tricks too and always appreciated these little private shows. It was always clear though that these guys were the real stars, we were just happy to be part of their evening.

We did a lot of work in these clubs. It was great. We performed at Lakeside in Frimley, The Stardust in Leicester, The New Cabaret Club in Newmarket, Caesar's Palace in Dunstable and Savva's in Usk, Wales. George Savva, by the way, was responsible for getting us started at these places. He was managing Blazer's when we met him – but went on to open his own top cabaret club – Savva's, of course.

George had a right-hand-man called Kevin King, who was often responsible for booking acts on George's behalf. He was very knowledgeable and experienced in the world of entertainment. I learned a lot about the industry talking to him, and to this day he remains a good friend. He's still heavily involved with the promotion of artists, particularly musicians.

Oh boy, I've got to tell you about Savva's and Freddie Star. Now Freddie, as you may or may not know, had a reputation for being totally crazy and completely unreliable.

In light of current media coverage concerning the behaviour of certain famous TV personalities from this time period I am aware of the fact that I may be playing with fire by relating this story. Sadly there will always be those who abuse their status as a celebrity to do things that they shouldn't. People who seem to bypass any kind of moral compass for their own end.

Freddie was mad, and saucy – but that was part of his 'act.' He was also very funny and fun to be around and entertainers could get away with a lot more sauciness on stage back then.

He was backstage throughout our performance, with Claudine in that now famous skimpy outfit, bare arse an' all – and Freddie would be standing in the wings opening the curtain for her as she walked on and off stage. He had this big, cheeky grin on and she was fully expecting him to do something naughty – almost reversing her way out through the curtain every time she passed him – but he never did! Which was surprising bearing in mind that he was pretty outrageous on stage!

After he had finished his show that night I went down to his dressing room. This colossal goon (sorry, minder) comes to the door and shouts for Freddie. Freddie appears and puts out his hand as if to shake mine – but then grabs my head in an arm-lock, like you see wresters do shouting 'It's the fucking magician!' He holds me there for a few seconds before suddenly letting me go and we get talking. I tell him about some of the shows we've done, including the stint at The King's Theatre in Glasgow where we met the stage door hand who was off to China to learn more about the martial arts skills he had acquired. He taught Claudine some self-defence moves that involve pinching a male attacker in sensitive places – other than the groin. (She wishes she had known these moves before.) It is very, very painful – I know this because she was keen to practice her new skills on me! Well Freddie can't wait to experience this for himself. I encourage him, perhaps unwisely in hindsight, to act out attacking Claudine from behind so that she can demonstrate her skills and so that he can feel the pain! So he launches himself at Claudine who proceeds with her pinching moves – putting as much effort into it as she can muster – but with absolutely no effect at all! Freddie's body is solid as concrete and she can't even pinch on the tiniest bit of flesh – he is literally all muscle. By now they're rolling around on the floor and then he grabs me again and *we* end up wrestling all over the floor of the dressing room, which was hilarious. Goon in the corner didn't flinch though. Perhaps it was just a normal after-show-in-the-dressing-room evening for him. Eventually we stop brawling and start talking again. He loves the act, he says, but thinks that when I take off my dark Terminator-style shades there should be these two huge eyes peeping out – cross-eyed though – which was a really funny idea. But no, I don't take his advice – it doesn't quite suit our act, I feel.

We worked on and off in the clubs for quite a few years, and those venues, without a doubt, were where our act was most suited. But what we didn't see happening was that these cabaret clubs were about to come to an end. The first shock waves hit the industry when Blazer's closed, and the rest of these fantastic clubs swiftly followed suit. It left a huge void in our lives. Our regular, hugely enjoyable work had come to a sudden end and we had absolutely no idea where we were going to go from here. It was a very abrupt end to an era, and a very sad one. And we strongly felt that true, live entertainment would never quite be the same again.

Just off stage at Savva's Nightclub in Usk, Wales. Hope you like my make-up! Claudine and I always enjoyed working with Billy Connolly

Chapter **18**

LIFE CONTINUED THOUGH. We had a few one-nighters here and there, and were booked to perform at the biggest yearly magic convention in the world: the Blackpool Magician's Society event at The Winter Gardens Theatre in Blackpool. Everything went pretty smoothly, but our act didn't quite register in the same way as in the smaller clubs. Some of our magic seemed to get lost in the vastness of this huge theatre. And we were somewhat upstaged by a famous illusionist called The Meretes. Hans Merete would perform a death-defying illusion that involved him balancing on a tube – in the same way as jugglers sometimes do whilst throwing their clubs in the air. But Hans had a bow and arrow in his hand and was blindfolded. He would fire the arrow into a target some 15 feet in front of him, which would in turn set off a sequence of bows and arrows that would each hit different targets. Then the final arrow would fire, slicing straight through the apple on the top of his completely dead still assistant's head – to rapturous applause. It was very dramatic and pretty dangerous – backstage we would all be ducking in case one of the arrows went astray and sliced through one of us instead!

But entertainment in the UK had changed beyond recognition and we were feeling disillusioned (haha!) and worried about our future as performers. We weren't ready to quit, we still had so many ideas and loved what we were doing.

Around this time entertainment agent, Chris Ferguson, became our personal manager and presented us with the opportunity in 1991 to take our magic to Zimbabwe. On first thought, we questioned the location – but it turned out to be, by far, our most enjoyable and successful experience abroad to date. Zimbabwe is a stunningly beautiful country and has some of the most breathtaking scenery we have ever seen. We were treated like royalty and were always given the finest hotel suites. We were able to order anything we liked from the menu – and my taste from long ago for lobster and fillet steak was resurrected! We visited Bulawayo, Victoria Falls and the country's capital Harare where our shows were very well received. Although a really rather worrying situation developed along the way; the locals thought I had genuine Black Magic skills, and despite being advised otherwise, continued to be highly suspicious of me – not believing me at all. I was just worried they were going to put some kind of evil spell on me, or lynch me or something.

When we look back at that trip and the spectacular beauty of the place, we realise how lucky we were to have been offered that contract. People pay a lot of money to visit Africa and to witness the safari parks and stunning sunsets, and we were spending our days enjoying all this for free – something we have never forgotten. One of our favourite places apart from Victoria Falls, was Lake Kariba, which for those of you who have visited this place, will know is an area of almost surreal beauty with incredible wildlife. We felt so very, very lucky to be there. Money, as usual, was always an issue – we'd got used to that on these contracts. The money we were promised never did materialise – we were paid in local currency – which wasn't really of any use to us (which sounds terrible but was true). There was the option to try and change the currency on the black market – but that carried the risk of being thrown into jail – which we were rather keen to avoid surprisingly enough! And with our luck with these foreign contracts – we thought it best to hang on to the local currency. But what were we going to spend it on? Everything was paid for. Let's just say that Claudine developed a taste for the local casino – and would often win and come back with even more money!

We heard about this guy: 'The Party Animal.' We were told to avoid him like the plague, that any contact with him would be at our peril. The people told us he was very a clever character – but we knew about 'characters' and had absolutely no desire to run into him. We got talking to a man – this unassuming, wiry little guy with big specs. He invited us to his place for the evening – a fantastic, huge sort of lodge. There was a colossal open fire burning and a drink was thrust into our hands the minute we arrived. It was at that moment that we realised that we had fallen prey to 'The Party Animal' and this was his lair. There was no escaping. What followed next was ludicrous. More and more people arrived and the 'games' commenced. There was 'bottle-walking' – don't remember much about that. 'Stool acrobatics' – where you had to crawl off a tall stool, through the bars of the stool and back onto the top of it without touching the floor – which, trust me, is far harder than The Party Animal made it look. Then there was the drinking. My God. Pints and pints of beer and then the challenge of running around the perimeter of the lodge in the dark, to then, drink more beer. There were penalties all night – that involved drinking whatever other people nominated you should drink. I was violently ill in the end. People were so drunk that I could show them that I was holding a lit cigarette in my hand, and much to their amazement – make it disappear before their very eyes – even though it was never there in the first place! Ah, the beauty of illusion! Anyway, by the end of the night we staggered back to our room. I looked in the mirror – I could not see my face. Now *that* is what you call an illusion!! And not one I care to repeat! So there you go, we had fallen foul of The Party Animal – who was the wiry be-spectacled little man we got talking to and the owner of the casino – it figures.

But all good things come to an end. All too soon we were back in the UK and to be honest, it felt really depressing after the fantastic time in Zimbabwe. We sat in our little rented flat with the cold British rain hammering on the windows (that had been repaired incidentally) – and tried to find the enthusiasm to put together a plan of action. We did not have the financial cushion of the club work anymore and pretty soon things started to get tough again. But never the types who give up, we spent the last little bit of our money creating yet another batch of publicity brochures – the best quality that we could afford – and sent it out to all and sundry. The front page this time was a shot of Claudine emerging from a wall of flames, with the slogan 'Our Magic is Hot.'

Before long we get an offer to work on a cruise ship. I laugh a lot when I hear that – when the telephone conversation had ended, of course! I'm asked if I've ever done any work on cruise ships before. 'No' I tell them. What on earth was I supposed to say, I ask you?! I thought it was the sensible reply! The booking is for a cruise company called Fred Olsen Lines, and the ship is named The Black Prince. It is still in operation today. As usual, nothing was cut and dried – it never was where we were concerned. Literally every contract we signed had some kind of twist to it and a developing horror story, and this turned out to be no different! Even the one-night bookings had always seemed to invoke a clash of fate or bad-timing, or whatever you want to call it. It would appear that everything we booked, even if it was six months in advance, and for a *single* night – seemed to be double-booked. Every date either side of the suggested day would be free – just not that day. This happened so many times that we actually began to wonder whether it was a coincidence at all, and whether in actual fact, my grandfather had a hold of our diary!

We accept the contract anyway and off we set for The Black Prince. But this we found out was no ordinary cruise – perhaps the clue we missed was the *'black'* in Black Prince! Fred Olsen Lines had decided to use the ship as a sort of mini-cruise come ferry-run as they wanted to break into the Danish/Scandinavian market. It was to run back and forth between Sweden and Copenhagen, in Denmark. This however, stirred up a lot of politics in both countries. Turns out both countries object to having a Norwegian ship sailing about in their waters with 'foreign' staff on board. It got so bad that we were strongly advised to not get off the ship at all when we docked. Or should I say, tried to dock – as there would be police lined up on the quayside in full riot gear, shields an' all – trying to control the hostile protesters that were waiting for the ship to arrive! Fights would break out and people would chuck themselves into the water to try to prevent the ship from docking!

Madness! The situation was not helped though by certain eggs that got thrown from the ship . . . in the end the situation got ridiculous. There were weeks when there were hardly any passengers on board, so us entertainers would just spend our nights (and days) getting pissed. We were getting paid anyway – but for doing very little now – and it got so boring, so we were forced to turn to drink! No surprise really that the contract ended early and we were sent home. The ship company said 'Nothing like this has ever happened to us before . . .' as they shook their heads in disbelief. Now how many times would we come to hear that? Kinda reminds you of Jonah and the big ship, don't you think – when he gets thrown off the boat because a huge storm kicks off the second he steps onto it. And the second they lob him overboard, everything calms down!

Once again we're back in the bloody UK. And once again the money we earned disappears faster than one of my own bloody candles. But now, and would you believe this – we are offered yet another contract in yet another country. This time in Japan. We pack our kimonos and go.

Chapter 19

WOW, JAPAN! What a place this was; expensive, culturally diverse, and down-right strange at times.

We were sent to perform in a place called Sendai, about a six-hour drive north of Tokyo. The hotel was in a very remote spa region. We stepped into an immaculate reception area flanked by huge glass panels. The Japanese are an intensely hospitable and polite race of people and we were immediately poured a drink. While we sipped our drinks we took a moment to take in our surroundings. On the other side of the colossal glass panels were spas and swimming pools – nothing strange about that. But we thought we were seeing things when we realised that literally everyone was nonchalantly walking around completely naked. One guy was laid out on the floor like the five of spades, to all intents without a care in the world. We discreetly looked away and then at each other. Had we been sent to a nudist hotel?

Nothing wrong with that on the face of it, but this was to be a very unusual audience indeed. We were required to perform two acts an evening, lasting about 15 minutes each. As I've said, the Japanese are extremely polite and always poured our drinks and did their utmost to make us feel welcome. But they spoke little or no English, so it was very difficult to communicate. A typical evening would go like this; the Japanese men would arrive wearing their kimonos, accompanied by their chosen Geisha girl – and promptly get drunk on Sake. Very quickly get drunk too. Many of them would be asleep in their chairs by the time we got to our second act, or would have left. We could understand them falling asleep – Japanese men work crazy long hours. But what we couldn't understand was this; those who stayed and were awake had this disconcerting habit of rolling on their backs with their legs in the air and pulling up their kimonos to reveal their testicles –

right in the middle of our act! Why? They seemed fairly oblivious to our presence apart from this bizarre ritual.

It was a peculiar set-up and this was quite strange behaviour, don't you think? It didn't make any of us feel particularly enthusiastic about our shows. As I've said, very little attention, if any at all, was paid to what we were doing. The days were very long and we couldn't really leave the hotel to explore our surroundings – this was a very remote area of Japan, remember, and there wasn't really anything outside to explore. I did try the spa once – now I like a hot bath – but this was excessive! It would strip the flesh off you! And it was very expensive; we had a food allowance of around £250 per week but that soon went, and had to use our salary to buy more food. I did get some work done on the floating chandelier though, I'd bought the materials with me to try to build it and had also thought up a way to make this potentially beautiful illusion work.

There were some Philippinos working with us in Sendai. Seems they really liked sex. Which I have no objection to whatsoever, I quite like sex myself – but I did object to the noise they made in their apartment (right next to ours!) every night! Bloody noisy they were. This singing, noisy duo asked me one evening if we received 'tips' for our shows. I didn't really understand, as the word 'tips' can have several connotations, especially in this environment, so I just told them we were professionals, not street entertainers, and that tips were not really part of our act; it was a little bit beneath us as it were. Too late I realised what they meant. I learned that this clever couple incorporated some close physical contact with their audience in their act, using their hands as they sang, and were being given quite sizable tips for this personal attention. I found this out on the last night of this particular booking.

As we were packing our props on this last night and preparing to leave the venue, the manager called us over. He managed to communicate a few words to us that indicated that there were a couple of guests who would like to meet us personally. He led us to a Japanese man and woman sitting in their kimonos to the side of the stage. The gentleman said the word 'Beer?' and we politely accepted, but realised it was going to be difficult to have any further conversation as we unfortunately did not speak any Japanese and they did not speak English. I did a couple of little visual tricks for them to break the silence, and they responded by giggling – and then he grabbed and squeezed her breasts and she squeezed him between the legs – to more fits of giggles. We found this quite funny ourselves, probably for an entirely different reason – and in truth – pretty alarming too! But we tried not to laugh – I certainly thought they might be hinting at some kind of foursome – and didn't want to appear to be encouraging this. I quickly followed with a few more tricks. To more giggles. And then they suddenly and silently stood up. The Japanese gentleman then reached into a leather bag and pulled out some crisp bank notes, which he laid before us on the glass table in perfect formation. They then bowed and left. We later found out that this was equivalent to about £300. The manager informed us that this was not unusual, and that the singing duo received tips of between £200 and £300 a night. No wonder they asked us if we received tips!!

Tragically, Sendai was hit by the 2011 tsunami and we don't know if that hotel is even there anymore. Visiting Japan, even for this short time as entertainers, was an incredible experience. We were very well looked after, a bit bemused about the response to our magic though, and at times utterly aghast at what appeared to be quite usual, but bizarre behaviour by the Japanese men! And if we ever visit again? Yes! But we do accept bloody tips!!

So we're back in Blighty again and back to enforced unemployment. This was always the sequence of events. But this time we're getting a very good name for ourselves with the entertainment agents and attracting even more interest internationally. We start to realise more than ever that our future does not lie in the UK – and even if our 'foreign assignments' always came with a strange, unwritten agenda – they were an education in themselves! And despite the enforced unemployment, we never stopped working –

always honing our acts and creating new ones. The floating chandelier too was now perfected and I was so happy with it. I made it appear first from a silk, and then after placing it on a hook attached to my elegantly designed magic table, using fluid, skilful moves that make it appear to turn and float around the silk. It is stunning to watch. The first time we use it – at a small magic convention for Edwin of Supreme – the response is wonderful, with members of the packed audience describing it as a 'beautiful.'

We get the chance to perform at some holiday camps in the UK, but we turn them down. Maybe it was arrogance, or just that we knew our act was better than some cheesy Butlins/Pontins show. I'd hated that whole holiday camp thing when I worked there as a kid so there was no way I wanted to go back there. It was sophisticated and classy Monte Carlo for us! Or so I hoped. We hadn't made it there yet . . . but you gotta keep dreaming, right?

Chapter 20

1994 – Hong Kong came next. A place called Kowloon. And Monte Carlo it certainly bloody wasn't. Maybe, in hindsight, we should have stuck to Butlins!

We spent weeks in preparation for this trip. We had to make all these plywood boxes for all of our equipment for a start – because professional flight cases are very heavy and sometimes create more hassle than they're worth due to weight restrictions and charges. The first thing that hits us when we arrive in Hong Kong is the intense humidity – we were literally dripping with sweat after about three minutes of landing – and they say only horses sweat!! We were taken through bloody filthy streets lined with filthier buildings; millions of blocks of flats and shops and businesses, all falling apart at the seams and so dirty. Our hearts start to sink – is this going to be even worse than Belgium? Was that even possible? You know what? It was. Our 'apartment' is shocking and I immediately tell the people responsible that we are absolutely *not* having it. After a huge verbal battle they finally agree to move us to another 'apartment.' This one is equally as horrific but the organiser has the cheek to yell at us, telling us not to 'trash it!'! I tell him that somebody has already done that for him – it's another total shithole, and stupidly expensive, like all apartments in Hong Kong apparently. But we had no choice but to take it.

We're becoming *seriously disillusioned* (sorry, had to get it in there again!) with where magic is taking us. I mean, is this it?? Every time we arrive back home people tell us how envious they are of our glamorous lifestyle; travelling all over the world doing what we love for a living. *Glamorous*?! Making a *living*? Sleeping on bug-infested mattresses with rats running under the floorboards?? Living hand-to-mouth paying extortionate rents to bleeding screwball landlords? Strangely though, we rarely ever shared the truth of our 'adventures' with anyone – until now. Particularly the undercurrent we felt from my grandfather. I guess we wanted them to believe the glamour and be proud of us.

They didn't see us heaving props across car parks, spending hours setting up and rehearsing until we were ratty and exhausted. They never heard about the nerves and stress before every single show and the terrible fear that something might go wrong, or the silent pleading that everything goes smoothly and according to plan and be well received. They just look at us like we're stars believing that everything is done for us; that we effortlessly waft onto stage – deliver a blinding set and waft off again to rapturous applause and adulation. That we stay in five-star hotels drinking champagne, wrapped in fluffy white bloody towels. Nothing could be further from the truth – well, for us anyway. That's the difference between us and amateurs. I don't want to sound bitter, but an amateur is tucked up in bed by midnight with his thumb in his mouth, while we're packing up props at 1am ready to be dragged out of sleep at 5am to get elsewhere. One minute in the freezing cold rain of the Falklands (or indeed the UK!), next in the sweaty, hideous humidity of Hong Kong after a completely thankless night of magic.

And thankless it was. We'd never seen or experienced anything quite like this in our lives. Never mind the accommodation, which was unbearable enough, but the venue was bordering on a joke. Why for fuck's sake, were we even here? Our show, if you can even call it that in this place, was performed in front of very few people. There was a cabaret stage, but these strange booths or rooms were arranged all around it so that hardly anybody could actually see the stage. Which didn't matter in one sense – because every one of these rooms had a big, flat-screen TV in it where the people could watch the shows. But it was so weird, because there was obviously no interaction with the audience and no applause at all. It's like they were all perfectly content to watch the 'live' show like it was just on TV, not live and just a few feet away from them. But that wasn't all. In this same venue there were all these private rooms that could be hired by wealthy Japanese or Chinese people, or whoever could afford them. They could be used for all sorts of reasons, as we found out – even Karaoke – but they were certainly not used for watching our magic. These rooms were pretty lavish and were usually occupied by rich businessmen, content with flowing champagne and the attentions of high-class hookers, for want of a better expression. The whole thing was nuts.

Then the management came up with a bright idea. They felt that in order to create more interest in our act – I should perform some close-up magic in these private rooms. Didn't seem a bad idea at first, especially when it was agreed that I would be paid extra money – and no small amount – for any room that was happy to watch some magic for just a short time; about 15 minutes. However, the reality of the matter was quite different. The last thing these people wanted to see was me doing some bloody tricks when they've paid good money for the room, the booze and the girls! Can you imagine? (Knock, knock.) 'Excuse me Sir ... Madam – (smile as peep around the door to be greeted by Lord knows what) – would you mind terribly stopping whatever it is you're doing in there and watch me perform a little close-up magic for you instead ... ?' I don't think so! My services, not surprisingly, were repeatedly and abruptly rejected. Whatever – we were still getting paid pretty well for performing in front of practically no-one every night anyway and gave up caring. They should have just bought (or even stolen!) my video and played that in the booths instead – for nothing!

So, to sum up Hong Kong – I like to tell people that it was a classy, lavish establishment, that money was no object and that our presence there was just a novelty. But in truth it was disheartening and frustrating. I heard later that the place was raided and closed down.

It left us with a dilemma really, all this disappointment. Were overseas contracts doomed? Despite our initial feelings that that was where we were meant to be? Were cruises doomed too? Were we destined to play holiday bloody camps for the rest of our days

I think the look on Claudine's face here on the stairwell in Kowloon says it all. And this is their idea of a luxury apartment!

What do you think about the luxury kitchen? The landlord said, "don't trash it!" Yeah . . . As if that was possible!

until we were dragged off stage in wheelchairs? Were we, just *plain doomed*?!? Undeterred though, as soon as we get back home we carry on rehearsing, buy more props and illusions (because we know that we have to keep developing and evolving our act) and then rehearse some more. We hear on the entertainment grapevine that the market for shows on high-class cruise liners was really growing. We decide to investigate this avenue again.

As luck, or something, would have it, we receive direct contact from a well-known agent based in France who books entertainment for cruises. In short, she has received some of our promotional material and DVDs, etc and likes our act – so much so that she is interested in seeing how our live performances are received by the French audience. She offers us a one-month contract aboard a small French cruise ship called Le Mermoz (Le Croisier Paquet).

We agree to the contract, and look forward to joining Le Mermoz. We feel instantly at home on this ship. It is quite an old ship, built in the 1950s – immaculate and very traditional with lots of rich, polished wood and large mirrors. The French passengers are quiet and respectful, and beautifully dressed. We are now ready for our first show, complete with our new chandelier illusion and other stunning, visual manipulations. Gone is the ripping off of Claudine's dress – replaced by new, classy costumes that won't give the refined and mature French audience a mass coronary.

Our first show is a flawless performance and we receive a very warm reception. Wherever we go the passengers make a point of saying, 'Formidable! (Brilliant!)' and it feels really good to be appreciated for my original skill of being a magician and illusionist again. We kind of miss the rawness and the drama of our previous acts in the clubs in the UK, but times change and we must change with them. Our act is so well received that our contract is extended to three months, then six months – and then a year. A whole year on a beautiful ship surrounded by classy, beautiful people, drinking fine wine and eating good food! Wonderful. Gone are the days of smoke capsules in floating balls, squirty, infection-causing coins and suffocating silks! And the fact that I don't speak French meant that I couldn't offend anyone voicing my opinions!

On a cruise ship, though, your every word and actions get scrutinised – people are desperate for a little bit of on-ship excitement and gossip. Before, I would have been happy to oblige – but now I knew it was important to stay out of the way and let the people remember you for your show – not your craziness. One regular VIP passenger told me that there was 'more class in [his] shoes than any of the other acts he had ever seen on board.' This went to my head a little, or perhaps he had just been unlucky! But either way, I rather liked that comment!

We got to see some amazing places in that year, we've always loved Europe – particularly France – but Thailand became one of our favourite places, and still is today. But like all good things, our time aboard Le Mermoz came to an end – and in truth I think we were ready to leave by this time. Plus there's always the danger of stagnating or staying on just for the security, but we had earned plenty of money and were looking forward to home and a good old-fashioned English fry-up believe it or not – at the end of the day all that lobster and fillet steak and fine wine can get a bit tiresome, you know! We also, more than anything, craved a good, hot curry, getting the Sunday newspapers and watching TV. Funny the things you miss! But they are important things in life, believe me, when you've been away for a long time.

Finally we were back home, and this time it felt good – but we couldn't have left the cruise ship without an 'incident' – it wouldn't have felt right! We'd had a whole year without anything dramatic or scary or loony happening – until the final week of our contract. Guess it kind of took the decision of leaving out of our hands really. Here's what happened. Onto the ship comes this gay French Canadian cruise director. Now I've got nothing against gays, French-Canadians or cruise directors – but he seemed to have something against me. He took an instant dislike to me, and a few of the other performers for that matter. So he starts switching the scheduling about. He changes our performance times to the days when the passengers have been onshore for a whole day – a horrible time. The passengers are tired and it's very late when they come back on-board after these tours, all they want to do is eat and retire to their cabins. They've had more than enough excitement for the day and they're not in the right frame of mind for any more. I'm not very happy about performing on these nights and tell him so. I don't remember his response but I think he must have irritated me a bit because the next minute I have my hands around his neck. I only do this when pushed, of course. I'm guessing I was a bit unhappy about his apparent attempts to sabotage my success on the ship.

Anyway, that was it, game over. But we made some great friends in that year and this single incident didn't in any way affect our future work on cruise ships. Almost immediately we were asked by Le Mermoz to join their Italian cruise ships; Costa Cruises. But first we needed a break and to fulfil a few other contracts.

With the nightclubs mostly behind us, we wanted to give our performances a classy feel for the cruise ships

Claudine looking after our babies! A shed load of props – just about to be loaded onto the ship

We have always had a passion for candles, flames and chandeliers;
hence you might notice our choice of book cover.
Mind you, we never did manage to conjure up
a chandelier that size!

Chapter 21

BACK HOME WE ate curry and fry-ups until they came out of our ears – we read the papers in bed and watched TV. It was heaven. Perhaps our luck was changing – for the first time we felt the presence of my grandfather less – or so we thought. But things are never always as they seem. We get another contract almost as soon as we've laid the papers down though – in Slovenia. And then we shoot over to Evian on the French/Swiss border and do some fantastic shows at The Casino Royal – which we absolutely loved. We were backed by a whole troupe of dancers who were brilliant and the shows were a huge success. We even got the chance to shoot another promotional video at The Casino Royal and from start to finish the trip was completely uneventful! Which is something to say for us!

In between these contracts we took some time out to just be us – make some day trips to places we'd always wanted to go, and have some weekends away too. We went to Cheltenham and then Ascot, and spent some time in Kingston upon Thames – which is one of our favourite parts of London. We had a weekend in the historic city of York and spent many weekends in Brighton – which we also love. It was great just to sit in a café and drink tea and watch the world race by. We felt more relaxed than we had for a long time. But much, much later on I discovered something. My father gave me box of cuttings that had been in the attic for years. And as we went through this box we realised that these were all places where my grandfather had stayed or lived – every single one of them – it was all listed in his memorabilia. And more than that; I discovered that he used to visit Jersey. He stayed in a place called Springfields – the *exact* same place in Jersey where I stayed when I did that summer season and where I met Claudine. Coincidence? I then ran into somebody who knew my grandfather well – he said my mannerisms are just like his were; the posture, the way I walk and wave my arms about a lot – just like him! And weirdly enough an aunt who I've rarely seen in these last 20 years, said that my handwriting is identical to his! She couldn't believe her eyes! And I couldn't believe my ears. All too spooky – but too true to ignore.

You can perhaps write it off as genetics or chance or whatever, but there was no denying that as time passed I was finding out more and more about my grandfather and how similar we were in many respects. I have never claimed to have his particular abilities though. My aunt, as well as my father and my nan helped me to create a clearer picture of him in my mind. That and seeing some of the beautiful images and letters and testimonials that had been hidden away in that box in the attic for years. He had been such an unusual man for his time. Just a few years before he would have run the risk of being committed to an asylum for being a clairvoyant and a foreseer of events. And whatever you may believe about such things, there was no denying that his work, or talent, or gift – or whatever you wish to call it – was very much in demand. People have a need to know things they don't know sometimes, if that makes sense – and he was able to help them. But maybe after his death his work wasn't done – and he felt he still had to inhabit this world too, to a certain extent. Which is why I've always had this huge sense of his presence wherever I've been in my life. And it began the moment I got into magic, but if I'm honest, even earlier than that. It started with an old photograph I found of him that I put in my room when I was a kid. In the end I couldn't have the picture in there anymore – there was always such an intense atmosphere in the room while it was there. And take the conversation with that friend a while back – the sudden unexplained smell of the tobacco smoke in the room – just as we were discussing my grandfather. When I later showed her a photograph of my grandfather, she shivered involuntarily. She studied the black and white photograph of this charismatic man for a long time. She took in his immaculate suit, his slim, perfectly manicured hands and intense eyes. And I suddenly found myself telling her more about him, things that fascinated me ...

My grandfather was the sort of man who could walk into a busy bar and there would be a sudden and instant hush. People would observe his spotless suit, his slicked back hair and poised cigar. But he was unaffected by this hush, he loved people and would immediately begin a conversation with someone by first buying them a drink. But this would be no ordinary conversation. He would suddenly turn to the lady, for instance, and say 'Your staircase has two turns and your bedroom is at the top on the right.' And he would always be right, of course. How he knew these things still baffles me. The conversation would then twist and turn through many subjects, until the point where he felt that perhaps he was delving too deeply. He would then bid the good people farewell and move on, leaving them stunned and often moved. He didn't believe in a spirit world, he knew there is a spirit world and sometimes his observations were a little too poignant to handle.

He would throw all these crazy parties in the big places he rented across London. My nan, who actually used to be one of the famous Tiller Girls, would accompany him to his shows, but would then retire to bed. But my grandfather would still be wired and head back out again – in search of people and life. For a man who so loved the company of people and appeared to love life, it still remains a mystery to me why he killed himself? He would invite all and sundry back to the place he was living and they would party and drink until dawn – but then suddenly he would change. He would clap his hands and the party was over. People never disputed him, they would just leave. And then he would descend into his darker self. On the day that he took his own life my nan remembers that it had been one of those nights. She awoke in the early hours of the morning to the sight of him standing looking at her in the dark, immaculately dressed, as always. She never saw him again. He left the house and never returned. He drove north to a hotel near Cheltenham, where he ground aspirin into a powder ... It took me some time to absorb this information;

Cheltenham – the very place that Claudine and I had visited so many times, the very place where my grandfather had taken his own life.

It was years later, when nan was living in modest bedsits, that she finally told me of the story of his suicide. But when she told me these things, it was without fuss or drama. She had loved him, but I got the feeling that he can't have been the easiest person to love. And when I found out about all those places that we'd visited or lived – the very same places where my had grandfather lived and worked – I felt that we were drawn to those places, that he wanted me to walk in his footsteps somehow, Cheltenham included. I keep an open mind on these things now, I have to. But I can't help but wonder – is there something he's been trying to tell me all these years? Something I've missed? Like I've said, I've never claimed to have his particular gift – I just know that I always loved magic. But I always come back to the same answer when I think about this – maybe he was in some way rattled by the fact I didn't acknowledge his presence in the early days of my magic. But I'm doing it now ... so I hope he's bloody reading this!

So then, back to the story! We're just enjoying relaxing for a while when we get an offer to perform for one night only for the President of Malta! Would you believe it?! The President! Wow! The agent in Malta explained that the President would be attending the opening of a brand new shopping centre in Malta called The Plaza. Lots of other events would be happening that day, fashion shows and music etc – but the agent had this idea of Claudine appearing from one of our illusions and handing the key to the President. It all sounded great so we devised a way of doing this.

One week before flying to Malta the agent calls us again. He says he needs Claudine to be fully dressed as the President is worried about being photographed with a young woman who isn't wearing very much! Well this presents a huge problem, as this particular illusion would be extremely dangerous if Claudine was fully clothed. I explain this to the agent, half expecting him to cancel the

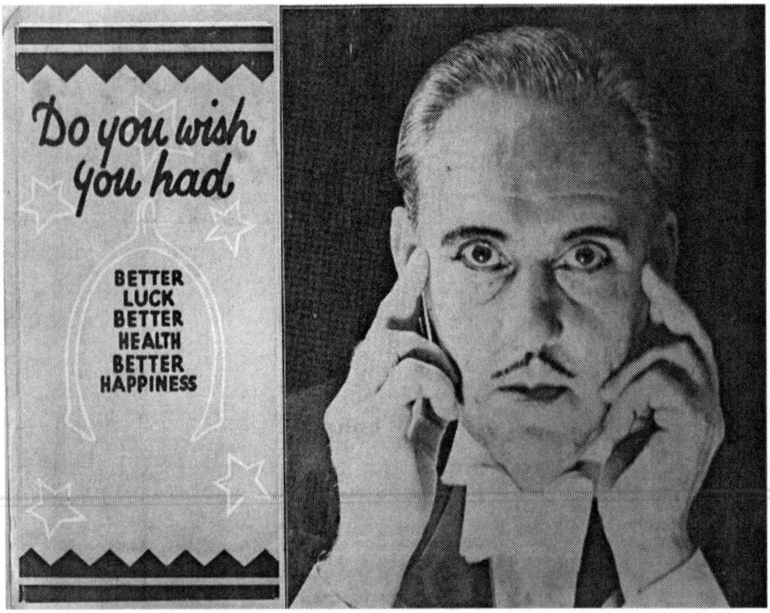

Look into the eyes! Here's my grandfather. What a great man.

contract. He calls me back – and tells me not to worry, that they've decided to present the key to the President in a different way.

So we resume our usual routine of boxing up the props in a way that means we can carry them – as we have the on-going issue of weight restrictions on the plane. Our flight is at 6am from Gatwick (great) with check-in at 4am (yuk). So we forget about sleep and leave at 2am (arrghh), imagining that we can perhaps sleep on the plane. But it's so bloody noisy that we soon give up on that idea. It's only a three-hour flight to Malta but with a two-hour time difference at the end – time is moving very fast – and we're aware that we need to get to the shopping centre and set up absolutely ASAP. There is the predictable delay in collecting our luggage when we land, before we finally meet the agent who takes us to our apartment. We check in and take the lift to the eighth floor to drop

Impressive memorabilia. Here's a clipping of one of his promotional pieces.

off our personal luggage etc. Thankfully the apartment in the hotel complex is clean and smart – single beds though – but all good. But our main concern now is getting to the venue and setting up.

The agent drops us there with all our kit and then buggers off. The scene that greets us can only be described as pandemonium, chaos, mayhem – any or all of those words – and blind panic. People are literally running about everywhere in this 'nearly' finished shopping centre. Walls are still being painted, for goodness sake! This isn't unusual in foreign countries, they seem to like taking three years to do anything and enjoy leaving everything to the last minute – but this was complete crazy madness! We kept asking people where the show was to take place and eventually found out that it was on the top floor. Okay. So the next question is – where can we find the lift? We ask again for help – with very little response from anyone. Eventually the floor manager shows up and tells us 'No lifts – they're not working yet. But they'll be ready for tonight.' I start shouting when he says we'll have to use the stairs. There is no way we can lift these heavy soddin' boxes up the stairs! So he calls over various workmen and they start debating in Maltese. The workmen look horrified. What on earth is the floor manager saying to them? He turns back to us, 'You can use the lift,' he says, 'but at your own peril as there is no floor in the lift yet' Brilliant. We drag all the gear over to the lift entrance and yep, he's right. The lift is working but has no floor, just a ledge around the edge about a foot wide. We have no choice really. So clinging on for dear life, plus hanging onto the props, we make our way to the top floor – staring certain death in the face as we climb higher and higher up the lift shaft. Holy, holy shit.

We're shaking when we reach the top, and dicing with death, inch our way around the edge of the lift and climb out. We take a look around. The place is just a shell, with bright, white walls. There are hardly any shops open and there still appears to be no stage. Where on earth and how on earth were we going to perform a show up here? As I've said before – magic needs mood and atmosphere and the right lighting – and it was so bright up here you needed bloody shades! Time is flying by now and we're sort of starting to panic ourselves. We ask again where the stage is and someone points to the escalators, so we go over to see. Well this is the flimsiest stage I have ever seen in my life, it appears to be made out of some kind of alloy – Claudine could have picked it up with one hand. But worse than that – it doesn't have a top. Yet again we ask about this new problem, but it's mayhem up there and the workmen all say at once 'It's coming, it's coming!' Eventually the boards arrive and are slung across the lightweight frame – but not secured. A ridiculously dangerous situation. Another thing they hadn't thought about was how on earth were we supposed to get onto the stage – it was four foot high! 'There are no steps and we have no way of getting any' came the reply when we asked. I have to say I started shouting again at this point. Claudine doesn't shout – but even she was starting to look vexed. The workmen fetch beer crates and try to make them into steps, but that doesn't work. Then they have the idea of bringing up some concrete slabs from the ground floor – by hand in the death-trap lift – and use these. We tentatively climb up the concrete slabs and step onto our stage. My God. One false step at the front and one of the plywood planks would flick up and bloody catapult you over the balcony to another version of certain death. This is a bad. But would make a great finale, don't you think!! But really – this is bad and we're seriously getting worried. Part of the illusion we are to perform in just a short time does involve me jumping and I just know it's going to be straight through the plywood or straight over the balcony for me.

We set up, treading carefully across the boards and then go to find somewhere to change. Which was a complete ordeal in itself as all the white walls seemed to have this fine, white, powdery residue all over them that found its way onto everything we touched. We were in black costumes – so you can imagine how that looked. We still haven't slept at this point so we're getting more and more tired. And then the show is delayed because nothing else is ready. We're ready to drop by now, but finally at 11pm it's show time. Nervously we walk on, worried that the floor is going to give way at any time, and precariously run through our show. There is very little response from the audience and hardly any applause – but the agent informs us that this is usual in Malta. Perhaps they would have reacted more had we fallen through the stage or flown over the balcony. But we don't feel good about it at all. We haven't slept for 36 hours, haven't eaten and we have to wait until the show ends at 1am before we can start packing up. Finally we head back to the apartment, stopping off for some food on the way.

It's about 2am when we take the lift up to the eighth floor and crash out in our single beds. Claudine is fast asleep in no time, but my mind is buzzing. I'm so tired I'm over-tired if you've ever had that – and I can't settle. I'm going over and over the performance in my head, questioning everything and wondering (with the odd blissful exception) why it is that every single bloody contract we get turns out to be crazy? Why can't they just run smoothly? Finally I nod off but within what seems like minutes hear this ENORMOUS *bang*!! But I'm so physically and mentally tired by now that I start questioning myself – did I actually hear the bang or is it my state of mind? Am I dreaming or was I having a nightmare? I don't even know, but I whisper to Claudine, 'Did you hear that bang?' But she is sound asleep, obviously she hadn't heard anything, so I nod off again.

Then I hear glass smashing and it's so loud it's like it's in the room. This time I know it's not my imagination, it was loud and clear. I lie there for a minute or two – knowing now that I am completely unable to sleep; I'm lying there waiting for the next unexplained noise. But I don't hear a thing. After a few minutes I tiptoe to the apartment door and peer out into the marble corridor. Everything is completely quiet. I'm going nuts I think. I get back into bed. Psychologically now I'm pretty wired and lie there in the dark feeling like shit. Five minutes later I hear the smashing glass again – only this time over and over again. I'm on my feet. This time Claudine has heard the noise, but she's still half asleep and not that interested. She wearily suggests that I phone down to reception to find out what is going on. Another huge smash of glass and I do just that, ready to give it to them with both barrels! But I don't get the chance, this is how the conversation goes ...

"What on earth is going on with all the noise?" I yell. And this is what happens ... there is complete silence followed by a man's terrified voice screaming ...

"Oh my God, Mister, get out, get out, get out! Oh my God, you die! The hotel is on fire! Get out! Get out!"

By now of course the adrenalin has kicked in, I'm not so tired anymore – funny how the thought of burning to death does that! I run to the door, shouting to Claudine, trying to drag my clothes on the way, and cautiously open it. The first thing I notice is the acrid smell of smoke and the second thing I spot is that there is glass on the marble floor. I look up and down and realise that all the fire extinguishers have gone from behind their glass covers – that was obviously the smashing glass that I heard. Claudine is by now rushing to get dressed and I tell her to wet the bath towels and bring them for protection. She is starting to panic. We run for the stairs but the smoke is so thick that it's hard to breathe. We wrap the towels around our faces, not sure what to do next. We suddenly see a door and make a dash for it. It opens out onto a raised mezzanine floor on the outside of the building and we see that everybody is gathered there. We join them. It is 3am by now and we are standing outside in the middle of a huge thunderstorm in Malta. Instead of burning to death, we're getting soaked. There are moments in your life that are so surreal that you actually wonder if you're dreaming them.

But this was no dream. It was another of our nightmares. We have to wait outside the hotel in the torrential rain, with thunder and lightning going off above our heads, until 6am. We are finally allowed back in, soaking wet but relieved to be alive. It's then that we find out what happened.

The night porter I spoke to on the phone – the guy screaming in fear – was one of those old guys who has been in his job for many, many years. He had this little routine of locking up and then sitting on a stool with a book, next to a reading light in the main hallway just by reception. That's how he spent his nights. The first bang that I heard could have been a very deafening clap of thunder, but I find out that it wasn't. It was what happened next that was scary and made us once again question why we were here and why this had happened. No, the bang I heard wasn't thunder – it was lightning striking the very top of the hotel. If the Gods (or my grandfather!) had wanted to make a point with a huge lightning bolt – then why not just do it when we were on our own on the way back to the hotel? Why did the lightning have to strike the hotel? It struck at the very point where the air-conditioning unit on the roof is connected to the very large metal shaft that runs the entire height of the building, from the ground floor to the vents on the roof. The bolt travelled all the way down this shaft, blowing a huge hole in the hotel lounge and setting fire to it. The night porter, who is quietly sat reading his book by a lamp in the dead of night, is blown clean off his stool. And guess what – when I meet him he tells me that he's never had anything like this happen to him before, poor chap. We don't tell him that we were pretty used to things like this happening to us.

As we make our way back down to what is left of the reception area to check out, desperate now to get out of Malta, we find out that the fire engines that were sent to control the fire didn't have ladders that were long enough to reach the top floor. So had the fire got out of control they could not have helped us at all. Comforting.

No matter, we have a flight booked back to London as we are due to attend a magic convention that day. We board the plane and sink into our seats – well, as comfortably as you can sink into a seat on a plane that isn't in first class, and we take off. The weather is still horrendous and the plane is jumping about a bit, but a bit of turbulence at most is a little disconcerting, nothing more. But suddenly, about an hour into the flight, Claudine turns to me and says 'There's something not right in here.' Now Claudine has always been the one who gets all the premonitions – I am just a conjuror who gets strange vibes sometimes. But she is the one who will mention someone's name – and then they call or turn up, or will say that she's worried about a friend and it turns out they have a problem and need help. So when she tells me that something's not quite right while I'm 37,000 feet in the air – I have reason to believe that I should listen.

Within seconds the plane jerks forward and starts to nosedive. All the oxygen masks drop down and all the overhead lockers drop open at the same time making a huge bang. This all happens in an instant and is immediately met by screams and shouts of terror, but some people are sitting in total silence, too shocked to react. I don't think a single sound came out of me and Claudine, we just grip hands. I don't remember thinking anything, certainly not anything emotional – but Claudine told me afterwards that she did think we were going to die together on that plane. The whole experience lasts no more than 20 seconds, but my God, they are the longest 20 seconds of my life. The plane starts to level out and then we realise we are banking hard to the right. It is then announced from the flight deck that we are having to fly back to Malta due to serious decompression problems.

Four hours later we are on another plane back to London, by now beyond exhausted after surviving 48 hours of no sleep, an exploding hotel and a nose-diving plane. And just to add insult to injury – we missed the magic convention. Just another normal contract for us then.

Chapter 22

MALTA WAS MAD. After that contract and taking into consideration all the crazy shit that seemed to happen on our other contracts – we now seriously started to wonder if cruise ships were a better option for us – even though they hadn't been without their fair share of dramas. In any case, what with the closures of the clubs and so forth, it was now becoming apparent that it was pretty much the only work available to us.

We were still under contract with our first cruise booker, who had mentioned work with Costa Cruise Lines. Turns out it wasn't as easy as we'd first hoped to get a booking with this company. The reason is that the companies who book entertainment for cruises are under orders to do so at the cheapest possible cost. Cruises, like everything, had changed – and they were trying to become much more competitive price-wise. A cruise was no longer the expensive luxury that only a certain calibre of society could afford. I hate to say it, but they were trying to go much more down-market in order to attract more custom. And along with that went the need to book much cheaper entertainment. They didn't want to be flying artists over from the other side of the world, along with all their equipment – when they could probably book something much closer to home for half the price. It was far more cost effective for them to book, say, a singer or a comedian with a single suitcase of stuff – than to pay for the both of us, plus all of the props we required now for our magic – they didn't want to do it anymore because it just cost them too much. Gone were the days when the class and glamour of a cruise went hand-in-hand with speciality acts like ours – and when money was no object. Sadly costs were being cut; everything had to be on a budget – and although we didn't feel the effect of this immediately – later it would become very apparent.

Finally though, we did join a Costa ship in Italy, and other Costa contracts followed. At this point we were still earning some of the best money on board. The problem with that was a lot of the staff knew this and there would be this horrible undercurrent of jealousy. We were being paid pretty well to do two short cabaret spots per cruise, whereas these people were up all hours slaving away cleaning or cooking or working in the bars and restaurants, basically catering to the whim of every passenger on board. They work very, very hard – of that there is no doubt. But it's completely different to the work we do. It's just worlds apart. They don't see what goes on behind the scenes, they don't know how hard we've worked to get to this point – they just see that we get paid a whole lot more than they do and it pisses them off. It doesn't make for a relaxed atmosphere and can get pretty wearing when you're out at sea for any length of time.

And the fire drills; the endless bloody fire drills. When you're on board for one week, the fire drill is just a temporary interruption of your beer on deck. But when you're on board for weeks – it's infuriately irritating. Once a week we would find ourselves on deck, listening to a bloody fire drill in what seemed like 90 different languages (because of all the nationalities on board) and getting more and more annoyed. Then the officer decides that he wants Claudine to do the lifeboat drill demonstration – I'm not joking. This is not really the way we want to be seen on board, as you can imagine. And we have no idea whatsoever why he wants Claudine to do it. She's not happy about this at all and stumbles through the whole thing in the 90 languages (5 languages really!), not sure of what she's supposed to be doing because, no surprise, pretty much the *last* language spoken in the drill is English. She's feeling a total prat and when it's over, is glad to just walk away. The officer is having none of it though, and proceeds to ask Claudine where the drill book is. 'In the cabin,' she replies, 'where it always is.' He then tells her, in his bullish, arrogant manner, that he is going to fine her because she doesn't have the book with her! She is furious! Especially as she feels one of the officers should be doing this.

As Claudine explains: '*Dean is fuming and goes on one of his mad searches to find the officer and give him what for. Somehow the whole ship gets involved – and they start looking for Dean. There are people shouting and marching about all over the place. Nobody can find Dean and Dean can't find the officer. Turns out the officer was also the ship's priest and we think the staff hid him so that Dean couldn't find him!*'

A bullish, arrogant officer/priest . . . now what can you say to that, I ask you?! Honestly though, the silliest things drive you nuts when you're on a cruise, or some other situation whereby you sort of feel trapped by your surroundings and not able to do anything about the things that drive you nuts. The air-conditioning was another thing. This endless, bloody stream of cold air in the cabins. Why?? Have it in the cabins as an option by all means – but don't inflict it on your passengers whether they like it or not! Some of us actually *like to be warm* believe it or not! I used to block up the vent with cardboard and cloths and tape – but the bloody cabin maids would report what I had done and it would be taken down – only to be put back up of course!

And the relentless tannoy announcements. Especially very early in the morning when the ship docks for a tour etc, and you've been up late the night before performing. And the silly, narrow single and actually pretty uncomfortable beds – again, okay(ish) for one week – but not for weeks and months on end. Makes you feel like you're away with your mate, not your wife; not very romantic. And the food – it was always delicious at the start of a cruise, but trust me – they don't change the menus and it gets very, very boring eating the same food week in, week out. Plus the restaurant times are very restrictive; if we were hungry after our last performance of the night (and quite often we were as there was a long gap between dinner and our last act) – we couldn't get anything to eat – which was actually really hard to deal with when you're hungry *and* tired. And you wonder why we craved a curry?! Sorry – must stop moaning and tell you some good stuff!! One good thing was that they didn't muck us about with money; it was always transferred monthly into our bank account and that was great – a huge relief – meant we knew our bills were being paid back in the UK and that our stuff wouldn't be out in the street when we got back!

Sadly it has to be said the Costa cruises we were on in Europe were not of the class and standard of the American Liners at the time, and although it was regular income – which trust me, was most welcome – we weren't completely happy with the declining standards. So when we got a call from an established agent in Monte Carlo (Monte Carlo? At last!) we were very interested, to say the least. He had booked illusionists before for his own shows on an American Cruise line called Royal Caribbean, and wanted us to be the star attraction of this production. We had heard very good things about this cruise line; it was one of the best in the world – and it didn't disappoint. We were an immediate hit and on the first night got a standing ovation – which was quite something apparently! The dancers, many of whom had worked with previous illusionists, told us that no other act they'd seen had received these ovations – so we felt pretty good about that. But it was to be short-lived. We heard that this company were not going to be using the agency in Monte Carlo for these production shows anymore, so what could have turned out to have been a few years work, ended after a very short period of time. I need to explain really how these agencies work; when this happens you can't just go and work for another agency on the same ship, because there are these little, hidden clauses in the contracts that say you cannot work for the same cruise company again, even with a different agent, for x amount of time – or sometimes ever again. We were gutted. People were shocked when they heard that our show was being pulled and were so disappointed. We had finally found our forte and it felt like it was being taken away from us – through no fault of our own – but because of these stupid clauses in entertainment contracts.

This same agent got back to us though and booked us aboard a much bigger ship as a 'solo' act – again for Royal Caribbean Lines. This was a huge ship. Really colossal. So excitedly we started planning and then working on a rather expensive, but spectacular illusion. We designed and then found someone to build this transparent pyramid that rested on top of a base that was about five feet high. It was fantastic. Claudine would climb some steps to pumping music and enter the illuminated pyramid. The audience could see her silhouette moving from side-to-side when suddenly I would cut the lights and immediately start thrusting spears into the sides of the pyramid. I would then deploy a hidden button that sent two pyro-explosions high into the air from the inside of the pyramid and the sides would drop down to reveal that Claudine had gone. The audience completely loved this, but the act wasn't over! I would walk to centre stage and point to the back of the theatre. The music would start again and Claudine would suddenly appear right there in the audience – which they loved even more – jumping out of their skins as she emerged blowing a whistle! What a finale! Would have been even more spectacular had we been able to use it more than once! Turns out that the agent hadn't quite communicated very well with the cruise company. You see the agent had told us 'the more spectacular the better,' whereas as the cruise director informed us that he only wanted us for ten minute slots – to be performed *in front* of the main stage curtains – which only gave us five feet of space to work with – or else we would have ended up in the orchestra pit. Again we were gutted. Here we were, aboard this immense ship – with this incredible pyramid illusion – and other expensive and spectacular illusions – that we couldn't use. It all seemed such a waste.

Once again the contract ended. We did later work for another agency on a different American cruise line – and met some guys who we really got on well with. They ran a magic shop in Miami and we met up with them regularly as we often sailed in and out of town. We had a lot of fun with these guys. One day, however, we found them in a deadly serious mood. They told us about a new series that was soon to appear on TV; The Masked Magician. This showed changed magic forever.

Chapter 23

THE MASKED MAGICIAN – what a thing that turned out to be. But before we go into that I've got to tell you about the American passengers on-board. We got fed-up with them if I'm honest, they would always use the same phrase 'Jeeeez … we lurved ya show!' So we'd say, 'Wow, thanks for that – what did you love about it?' But they never seemed to know. They never really seemed to want to take the conversation any deeper and would just reply 'We dunno … but we lurved ya show, anyway we are off to the midnight buffet!'

We did have some funny things happen on this cruise though, despite the Americans, the food, the air-conditioning and the hours and hours of boredom.

We liked to perform this trick that magicians call 'Smoke in the Glass.' In those days everybody smoked – it was long before the ban and I often used cigarette manipulations in my shows. I think I said before that these were some of my favourite tricks; I loved the reaction of the audience as I made them appear and disappear and re-appear at will. We used this one trick, Smoke in the Glass, quite a lot. It involved a simple coaster, a large brandy glass and a silk that Claudine would bring onto stage. She would place the coaster over the rim of the glass, and I would take the silk from her, covering the glass and the coaster. I walk to the other side of the stage, smoking a cigarette and blow the smoke in her direction (she doesn't thank me for that, incidentally). She then removes the silk and the coaster from the glass, which has now, by all accounts, filled with my cigarette smoke. The audience always loved this simple, little trick – and there are many ways that this can be done. Back then though it was done using two different chemicals – and I'm going to tell you how – you *need* to know how, trust me. One small drop of one chemical is placed in the brandy glass, the second small drop of the second chemical is placed in the centre of the coaster. So obviously – and hopefully you've worked this out already – when the coaster is placed over the glass, the chemicals fuse together causing a reaction of smoke – bingo! What appears to be cigarette smoke billows from the glass – and the audience are suitably impressed.

For Claudine however, this is not an easy trick to set up backstage. Firstly there is the worry of breaking or damaging this extremely fragile glass, but also there is the issue of preparing the chemicals. It has to be done literally seconds before she comes onto stage for two reasons; one is we do not want the chemicals to evaporate before she comes on stage, and the second one is – the chemicals are so powerful (which is why you only need the tiniest drop of each) that even before the coaster is placed over the glass they start fusing in the air – and the glass starts to cloud over before we're ready! The timing is crucial and Claudine would often be frantically cleaning the inside of the glass before she walked on with it. She got tired of dealing with the stress and insisted after one close-call with this particular trick that she wasn't going to perform it again until we'd worked out a different way of doing it.

The show ends and we go back to our room. We have two big bottles of these chemicals in our cabin and she suggests we just get rid of them. Without thinking I unscrew both bottles and proceed to empty them down the sink. At the same time. What the hell was I thinking? Well fuck me if this mini nuclear bomb mushroom-shaped smoke cloud doesn't bloody go and explode in the sink – instantly filling the whole cabin with thick, dense fumes!! Claudine hits the floor (by now, her learned reaction to these little incidents) and I run the taps as fast as I can, trying to wash the chemicals down the sink, but it's too late – the smoke is pouring out of the sinks in all the cabins in our corridor – and from every other vent and place that it could possibly escape! Everybody is convinced there is a fire but can't work out where and starts running around all over the place. Someone calls the captain. But by the time he comes down the smoke has dissipated. He looks at me suspiciously. But he can't pin the blame on anyone, so we sort of escaped that one.

It doesn't end there though as a couple of days later we have another little 'accident.' We're in our cabin again and I'm playing around with this trick that involves using magician's flash paper. This is paper that has been impregnated with yes, you've guessed ... chemicals ... so that when you light it you get this fantastic huge flash – and the paper evaporates. Well I had a load of this paper with me, enough to last four months on board, which I keep in a plastic box. So I'm practising this trick, lighting little bits of the flash paper and monitoring the result. Thing is, I've left the lid open on the plastic box and this one little piece of paper sort of floats off towards the box and well ... lands in it really. What follows is akin to a rather huge supernova going off in the corner – like the sun exploding in a very confined space. This time we both hit the floor. All the smoke alarms go off at once in our cabin and we realise we've only gone and blinded ourselves as well from the huge flash. Suddenly the phone rings and we're groping around trying to find it. I answer it in the most normal voice I can muster; it's the captain, asking us what is going on in our cabin. There's a strange sort of smell in the room now as well, a sickly sort of burning smell and as we struggle to see through our blinded eyes, we realise the whole cabin is covered in a strange, black chemical residue too. 'Ever so sorry,' I lie, 'We stupidly lit a match in our room ...' but I don't think he buys it. Thankfully though he doesn't decide to pay us a visit – Claudine is desperately trying to remove the black stuff off the walls and furniture in case he changes his mind – and the call ends. We think that we've got away with it again. We finish cleaning up the cabin and go down to dinner. But talking to the captain later though, I realise he suspects that both this and the previous incident with the smoke have everything to do with us.

Well I just figure that practice makes perfect. All of our acts are by now flawlessly executed. Better to blind yourself and singe your own hair (yes, that was the strange smell) and conduct chemical mayhem in your own cabin than inflict such drama on your audience!

We spend several years working on these cruises. It's a great way to see the world, but bloody hell – it gets so boring. Apart from rehearsing our acts or performing our acts there is little else to do. We were constantly worried about our props. Despite the colossal size of these ships, there is very little space to store anything much larger than a bloody mouth organ back-stage. I think this is why they didn't want acts like ours on board anymore. There was simply nowhere to keep our rather large amount of props. We had to store them literally anywhere we could find. We even used the carpenter's workshop once; not surprisingly everything ended up covered in sawdust. Another time we had to store them on the actual deck of the ship – they were boxed up but were still damaged by the salt that crept in through the gaps in the packaging. These are not cheap props and it was not easy, or indeed possible sometimes, to make repairs.

The politics and gossip on the ship are mind-numbing too. Most of the other performers spend their days locked in their cabins afraid to come out, for fear of saying the wrong thing or being misquoted or causing offence in any way. This may sound ridiculous but it's completely true. But I can't stay in the cabin – ever heard the expression 'cabin-fever?'! Well let me tell you it's a horrible thing. I had to get out and mix with some people, despite the threat of pissing somebody off. I would do a little close-up magic for them, or just chat with them. The rest of the time was spent sleeping or eating or drinking scotch. You had to drink scotch to sleep anyway – to drown out the incessant sound of the engines! It was starting to get us down. It wasn't what we wanted to be doing anymore. And don't get me started on the endless diarrhoea.

We were once informed by 'elf 'n safety (how nice of them) – that bacteria is rife on cruises. Claudine was often ill, more often than me – and we wonder sometimes if the illness she still suffers from now is a direct result of all those years on cruise ships. As you know, we often raided the kitchen at night – lots of the staff and crew and entertainers did. Because they were often working (and in our case, rehearsing) long after even the midnight buffet had been served. We got seriously hungry. The problem with that was that it was after-hours as it were – when the stringent health and safety procedures were not enforced. We literally wandered in and out of the kitchen without the protective clothes or hair-nets or gloves on. So even the slightest bit of bacteria could go rampant in an environment like this – affecting loads of people (not that I'm trying to put you off cruises or anything!) But even when these strict health and safety rules were applied, things still went wrong. There was one such case when nearly the entire ship had to be evacuated due to eating sword fish that had not been stored at the correct temperature. Literally hundreds of people were ill. Well, shit happens, as they say. Especially on cruises.

Chapter 24

SO ONCE AGAIN, and I apologise if this sounds awful – but we found ourselves getting seriously bored of cruise ships, in fact my favourite saying was by this time 'A ship is just a prison – with a chance of drowning!' But we still needed to earn money and were still being offered contracts. The Monte Carlo agent called us yet again – offering us a three-month contract with Princess Cruise Ships – departing from Dover. So we pack up all our props into a hired van and set off. When we arrive we meet up with the cruise director who immediately asks to see our props. He then goes on to inform us that there was no way there was room for this amount of equipment on board. We're fuming and have no choice but to get back in the van and drive home, stopping only once on the way to pick up the bloody exhaust. It fell off driving up those steep Dover hills.

I wanted our money for this cancelled contract, or at least some other suitable work and said so, but the agents were not keen to get involved. The agent will always side with the company; their loyalty undoubtedly lies with those who pay their commission. And I was told in no uncertain terms '*Do not* upset the company!' However, the agent did admit that the company had seen the DVD that featured our illusions – but that they still wouldn't acknowledge they had made an error of judgement regarding our props. By this time I had well and truly had enough of this Monte Carlo agent and seriously thought about suing them for three month's money. I was told by a solicitor though that it would be an extremely long, expensive and difficult process, because both the agent and the company were outside of the UK. I was furious and it didn't stop me from threatening them. But defeated, we just sat down and said 'That's it. We're never working for a cruise company again.'

The phone rang. It was only the bloody agent in Monte Carlo again. He offered us a short contract – just six weeks – on board another Princess cruise ship. 'What the hell,' we thought, and went. It turned out to be the worst cruise we had ever done in every single way. It took boredom to a whole new level. Claudine was very, very ill and desperate for the whole ordeal to end. It was at this point that we looked at each other again and said; we would never set foot on another cruise. But again, the decision was taken out of our hands.

Back in the UK Claudine failed to recover health-wise. She struggled for months to eat and would often have to rush to the toilet more than 20 times in a morning, sometimes passing blood. She was so drained and ill and after eight months of visits to the doctor, was finally diagnosed with Crohn's disease. It was a relief to find out what was wrong but awful to find out that there is no cure for Crohn's; it is a malfunction of the immune system whereby it over-reacts to bacteria – stripping the body of all good bacteria and creating terrible inflammation and agonising ulcers in the intestines. We wondered whether all the travelling had caused the disease, all those times she was so sick on the cruise ships. Claudine was given huge amounts of steroids to help calm the inflammation. She started to feel better, but as we all know – one of the awful side-effects of steroids is weight gain – and Claudine hated this after all the years of considering herself to be plump, and all the years of battling to stay thin and getting so ill with anorexia. It was a horrible time for her. In the end, she was prescribed a new drug; Infliximab, that hadn't yet been trialled in the UK. It worked brilliantly. We always knew it wouldn't be a cure, and that there would always be flare-ups – but finally Claudine started to make a recovery.

Our life had now changed dramatically. Claudine's illness meant we were completely unable to perform at this time. It's now 2001 and once again we find ourselves in a situation where we simply do not know what to do next.

Chapter 25

IT SEEMS LIKE a strange choice for us, I know, after all the years of travelling as entertainers, but we decide to get into property renovation. It's bloody hard work but we throw ourselves into it completely and become pretty good at it actually! We really enjoy the creative side of it and even manage to make some money along the way too – always a good thing. We're also finding the time to take some trips over to Europe, relaxing this time though, not working. We particularly enjoy visiting Paris and seeing all the shows; The Lido de Paris, The Crazy Horse and Moulin Rouge. These are sexy, glamorous shows and we love them. They quite often feature a wonderful speciality act or a classy magician – and our thoughts are never far away from the possibility of putting on our own shows over here. We love the sophistication of the acts; so classy and visual, thought-provoking and different. Audiences in England just don't seem to have the same level of appreciation for the beauty of these shows, and we find this so frustrating. And anyway, we are more than aware of the fact that we no longer have any real foundation in entertainment anymore, having not performed regularly for quite some time now. We then find out that even if we wanted to work again on cruises (which we most certainly don't) – we would be expected to pass a strict medical for insurance purposes. We know that Claudine would not pass this medical now, even though her health had improved.

We had strangely ended up moving to Northamptonshire in the year 2000 – in short we needed a larger property to house our magic props – and couldn't afford anything in London. We didn't want to sell them as we weren't convinced that our days of entertaining were completely over. We are more relaxed now than ever before, and Claudine is enjoying indulging her passion for cooking. We always did this when we were in London, even when we were in and out of the country working, but it's easier for her now that we are at home a lot more . She loves holding dinner parties and making everything really great for our guests. She likes to spend ages choosing food and going to a lot of effort presenting it in a tasty and beautiful way. Our friends love Claudine's cooking – but we never get invited back to their houses – they all say the same thing – 'We can't do it as well as you, so we won't try!' Sad really.

We have this idea to open a restaurant in Northampton. Claudine can use her cooking skills to best effect and we will only open to the public in the day, leaving the evenings free for private magic events or small shows. It seemed like a good idea on paper, but in hindsight it wasn't one of our best. It was very, very tiring and you need to be really busy all the time in order to make any money! The restaurant seated just 35 people and we quickly realise that although it's bloody exhausting, we're actually really good at running the place. Claudine's food is superb and we end up supplying local companies with buffets and holding magic-themed evenings called 'Magic by Candlelight.' These evenings were a huge success, people loved them, they'd often hug us when they left and tell us what a fantastic night they'd had – but my God, they were hard work. We'd always dress the restaurant for these events – and being a perfectionist everything had to look beautiful, with red drapes and candelabras, of course. I'd bring in another magician to act as compère, and together we'd entertain our small audiences with little talks about our lives as entertainers and obviously do some magic for them. Claudine would be slaving away in the kitchen cooking delicious food (so much for only opening in the day!), but the problem we had was that we'd have to clear the restaurant by 11:30 – and the people never wanted to leave! They'd often stay until 1am – and when they did finally leave the place would be in one hell of a state and need clearing up before the morning. Claudine's health started to suffer again and she ended up completely exhausted. The other unfortunate problem that arose was that a few young, local magicians started popping in for chats – which was lovely until we found out they were going away and gossiping about us, saying some pretty horrible stuff. I've never understood this kind of behaviour and find it very annoying. Anyway, we realised we could no longer carry on working at that pace, despite it being a success, and we sold the place. Time for a new venture!

Chapter 26

I NOW SET UP a company called Wow Entertainments. It's specifically for magicians really, and I don't do too badly to begin with – organising bookings for various magicians and illusionists. However I quickly realise that perhaps I am not the best person to be doing this; I am very proud and respectful of my art and discover that some of the fees that are being offered for some of the acts are ridiculously low. On the flip-side of that there are acts that are willing to sell themselves very cheaply just to get the bookings – which also doesn't do anyone any favours at all.

I am approached by a woman who is the main cruise booker for a Norwegian company. She also deals with other entertainment agencies and asks me to find her some illusionists for her cruise ship, which I do. Just to explain; the difference between a magician and an illusionist is that the latter will nearly always have a whole pile of large props – like the sawing in half of women, etc, etc – you will remember this from our experiences with our own props. Well despite the fact that this is what she's asked for – low and behold I start getting the same grief about these guys having too many props – just as we used to get! Or, that they do not have enough material to fulfill the contracts – because these companies are now demanding unreasonable lengths of time for their slots on one hand – but restricting the amount of equipment they can bring on the other. Lunacy.

The final straw that broke the camel's (or magician's!) back was this; I watch this young illusionist's DVD and it's pretty good. He has some good material. He still has a lot to learn, but he's enthusiastic and I think that he has potential. Everyone has to start somewhere, right? A bit like what Henk saw in me all those years ago. This kid has never worked a proper cruise before, and this Norwegian company is not the best in the world – so perhaps it would be a good start for him. I spent hours (too long really) talking to him on the phone, sharing all my worldly experience (!) and telling him what to expect on board. Eventually all the 'I's are dotted and the 'T's crossed and he's all signed and sealed to begin his very first contract on a cruise ship. We've even checked the small print in respect to end of his contract, which stipulates that he cannot work for another agent for a one year period; which is very generous in fact – because as I have said before, most agents insist on a life-time work agreement if they have introduced you to a company – which is actually crazy, but we won't go into that.

I then hear from the booker for the cruise company that he is struggling to perform effectively – not having quite enough material for the last show. But he does okay and when his contract ends it hasn't gone too badly for him. But he rings me many times asking for more work and I tell him that although I am putting his name forward, ultimately it's up to the booker from the cruise company to make the final decision as to whether they book him. But this young chap seems desperate and calls me again with the news that another agent can get him on board this same cruise ship but for less money. This puts me, as his agent, in a very difficult position. Surely the cruise booker understands that they can't book this same act through a different agent? 'Wrong' she informs me – she doesn't care what agent now represents this act so long as she gets the booking fulfilled! I find it hard to believe that both the cruise booker and this young lad, who I tried to help, simply have no morals – and it leaves a bad taste in my mouth. I then find out that the booker used a regular agent before he got in touch with me. This agent had left the scene for a while – but he was now back – and the lad had no problem jumping straight back into bed with him, so to speak. It proved to me once again how unscrupulous these agents and entertainers can sometimes be, and I decided I didn't want anything more to do with it. I wound the thing up.

But in the meantime, Claudine and I had got a few more bookings in France – which as you know, we loved. But we are now of the mind that our type of act couldn't really be taken anywhere anymore – and we had to sit down and decide once and for all what we were going to about that.

We do get this booking in Scotland though, which sounds fantastic. We check out the venue; The Turnberry Hotel in Ayrshire, and find out that it's a very prestigious venue to work. We decide to drive up there in our 4x4 and it's a beautiful bright, crisp day as we load up the car. It's a long way, but the weather is good and we're not in any great rush. We've arranged two nights at the Turnberry Hotel and the show is not until tomorrow night; New Year's Day. After about eight and a half hours on the road though I'm getting tired, the sun has now gone down and we're driving cross-country through windy roads trying to find the hotel. It's at this point that we unfortunately take a wrong turn. The road starts climbing higher and higher through a forest, it's pitch black and by now the infamous thick Scottish fog has descended – making my eyes and head ache as I try to follow the road. Claudine mutters that she thinks we are lost – and in my tired and bad-tempered state this is not what I want to hear. So I jam on the brakes and pull over, I am shattered and the last thing I want is to be bloody lost up here in the middle of bloody Scottish nowhere. We have no alternative but to turn around and go back the way we came.

So I swing the steering wheel around really hard and in my annoyance now slam my foot on the accelerator. This is where I learned the hard way that 4x4s are not sports cars. 4x4s have a tendency to be top-heavy (particularly when they are loaded up to the rafters like ours), and they do not have the benefit of a low centre of gravity or the turning circle of a racing car. You realise I'm just trying to make excuses for what happened next, don't you . . .! Well the left-side wheels of the car slide over the verge of the road, and I cannot pull the steering wheel round quickly enough when I take the turn – the momentum and weight and speed send the car flying over the edge of the ravine. The sounds are sickening as the car lands and then bounces and slides its way down the embankment, crashing into God knows what on the way. It finally comes to a stop on its left side pointing straight down the ravine . . . the headlights are still on and the back wheels are spinning. It is a terrifying sight. Claudine is crying and her left shoulder is very painful where it has been thrown against the car window, and we are both horribly shocked. As we carefully climb out of the right side of the vehicle – which thankfully we were able to do – all we can see is the thick fog around us, but little else. Apart from the headlights facing down the ravine, it is totally dark and very cold, we are quite high up and the wind is picking up. We decide we need to climb back up the embankment, we have no phone signal and besides, we don't even know where we are – how could we even give a location to the emergency services? We start scrambling up the hill and realise that we have actually been very lucky – we've only fallen about 70 feet. We wait by the side of the road, shivering in the dark – but there are no vehicles at all. There is an awful eerie feel in the air, and a deep silence that is only broken by the strengthening gusts of wind. I realise I may have to walk back the way we drove to get help – which could take a very long time. Claudine is very upset, she can't face walking all that way, she can't go back to the car and it is so, so cold on the side of the road. Just as we were beginning to panic a little bit, we see some headlights in the distance.

A car slowly approaches and I have no choice but to step out and flag it down, there is an older lady behind the wheel and even though I try not to startle her – she looks frightened as she gingerly winds down the window. I assure her that I am not a madman (?!) and explain what has just happened. She doesn't hesitate and tells us to get into her car. She drives us to the nearest house, which is miles and miles away. As she drives she explains that she only makes this journey once a year, to visit her daughter and that over the years she has never seen another car on this isolated road. Eventually we arrive at a house in the middle of nowhere, all the lights are on and as we approach the front door we see through the window that a table has been laid out with two puddings and two glasses of wine – all ready for the new year celebration. We are greeted by the sound of large dogs barking and when this women answers the door she seems to know instinctively that we have had an accident. She shouts to her husband who immediately pulls on his boots, asking where the accident happened. The wonderful lady who stopped for us has been clever enough to clock the distance we have travelled and tells him that it is precisely 13 miles back down the road. We later find out that this is in fact, the closest house for miles in this remote area.

We climb into his truck, which is fitted with a winch. He is a man of few words, but says in short that he doesn't think it will be a problem to pull our car back onto the road – but I'm worried – it's stuck in a really terrible position. He has helped others before, he says, and that this is a notoriously bad area for misjudging the bends. We say nothing. We're just so grateful that he is willing to help us.

Finally we arrive at the point where our car left the road. We peer through the thick fog and he mutters that we're lucky to be alive. He then climbs down and attaches the winch to the car. It has no effect whatsoever. We notice the eerie feel in the air again and watch, feeling helpless, as he struggles to haul the car up the embankment. Eventually he gives up, saying that this has never happened to him before, and pulls out his mobile phone. He looks at it closely and frowns, muttering that he doesn't understand why he hasn't got a signal. We suggest that it could be the fog, and tell him that we haven't got a signal either. But he has lived here for years, he says, the fog is normal and he has never lost his mobile phone signal on this network. So unable to phone for back-up we get back into the truck and he drives us back to his house, there is nothing left to do. He grumbles about his cold pudding on the table and we apologise. We continue the journey in silence. Suddenly, without any warning, all the lights come on in the interior of his truck and this poor man's actual words were 'Christ Almighty, WHAT'S THAT?!?' He cannot turn them off either. He gives up – needing to concentrate on the road – the last thing he wants is for his truck to crash too. After about ten seconds they turn themselves off and we look at each other in the dark. Please, no more tonight, we think.

Calls are made to various recovery firms, who all struggle to locate on a map where our car actually crashed. Eventually one firm agrees to come out, but they have to close the road and use a really big truck to pull the car out. It is an absolute mess and looking at it, and the location where we crashed, we realise that we are indeed very lucky to be alive. But even luckier to see the lone headlights of a lady who makes that trip on that remote road just once a year.

Looking back at this whole episode, we have to acknowledge the strangeness of it all – but not just that – what still astonishes us is the kindness of that lady who stopped that night, and the willingness of these complete strangers to help – without drama or fuss. In the midst of the horror of it all, we were touched by this man who gave up his pudding and glass of wine and without question, just did everything he could to get us back on the road. The car was in such a mess (to the sum of six grand in the end), but with the help of the mechanics we were able to get it going again. And if by some miracle, our props didn't appear to be damaged, and we were not dead or terribly hurt. We slowly drove back down that crazy road and got on our way to the hotel. It was a shame to pull up at that beautiful venue, screeching and scraping in such a mashed-up vehicle, with mud splattered all over it and bits of tree sticking out the bonnet.

We walked into reception to quite a reception. But then we must have looked awful. We too were covered in mud and completely exhausted. After getting cleaned up in the beautiful room they had waiting for us, we went back down to have a proper look at where we would be performing the next night. They explained that they're relying on us to put on a good show – because last year they booked a Shirley Bassey impersonator who by all accounts wasn't very good. Problem was they'd omitted to say she was an impersonator and everybody was expecting the real thing – so they were on a downer before the poor woman even opened her mouth – so she didn't really stand a chance!

We then explained what had happened that night. I wasn't in the best mood – having discovered on top of everything that some of our props had actually been damaged. They wanted to know briefly what we would be performing that night – and I described one of the new illusions that we were going to use that involved fire. The hotel manager immediately said he wouldn't allow me to use it – I told him I hadn't burnt a hotel down for a least a year – but he still insisted that I couldn't use it. I'm afraid he then got the blunt end of my tiredness and the after-effects of what had just happened to us. Anyway, the show was a success and we got a great response from the audience – so it wasn't a total disaster.

The next day it takes us 15 hours to drive the nine-hour journey home and we're back to cursing the whole way down the bloody M6. One of our young friends, Danny Boy, can't believe it when we explain what happened to the car. He comes up with a new name for us ... So we feel compelled at this point to raise a glass to the kindness of one Scottish couple, the old lady who came to our rescue and to our new stage name, 'The Deans of Doom!!'

Chapter 27

I AM SOMETIMES ASKED to present lectures as well as magic, and on one particular occasion in 2005, I'm invited to a magic gala in Milton Keynes as one of the main performers – since I have been asked to close the show.

My lecture is scheduled for around midday and there is a very good turnout for the event. I decide that in addition to me demonstrating the manipulation skills used for coins, cards, balls and thimbles etc, I will touch on the various travelling experiences in our lives as entertainers. I do my best to keep the stories upbeat – really I do – but then I realise that perhaps these magicians might not entirely appreciate hearing the cold facts of being a professional performer!

Anyway – who should I run into after the performance but none other than Joe Pasquale. I'm sure most of you know who I mean – the squeaky-voiced entertainer who won 'I'm a Celebrity – Get Me Out of Here!' I know Joe well, I'll tell you why in a bit – but it's good to see him and I ask him if he saw my lecture. 'No,' he says. But I need to know what the other magicians think (feedback is always useful!) so I ask Joe to ask about and let me know. 'Yeah mate,' he squeaks, 'I'll do it, but if you were kak (whatever that means – but I can guess!) I'll tell you, you know!' Later on I meet up with him again. I want to know what he's heard. He's only asked one person, he says, and no, they didn't want to know how fucking hard the business is. They just want to know how the chandelier trick is done and where they can buy it for £5! That's honestly the truth! I still laugh my head off when I think about that!

I forgot to mention that I met Joe at the time I met Claudine, when I was performing in Jersey. We used to hang out and play pool together. And all these years of fame have not changed him one bit, he is just one of the most genuinely lovely, down-to-earth guys that you could ever wish to meet. People ask me if he speaks with that squeaky voice in real life – well kind of – but I think he exaggerates it a bit for his stage performances. Joe, Claudine and I did this one-nighter at a place called The Pyramids in Southsea, Portsmouth. We hardly earned any money, but a gig is a gig, right. Joe did this really funny routine involving these huge church candles that blow up on stage – hilarious.

Anyway, a few weeks later we get a call from the same agent wanting us both again. Strangely enough, apparently they were going to book Shirley Bassey – but after seeing the two of us, decided to book us instead. It was for this big corporate do and they'd literally spent thousands getting the venue ready; the place has been totally transformed in preparation for this luxury event. Whilst we are getting ready to perform, Joe and me can't believe the transformation of the room compared to last time – and we're still on the same soddin' fee – so we both get completely ripped off! Something that had never happened to Joe before! Joe always reminds me of this story and tells it so funnily that we always laugh our heads off – God knows what the agent creamed off of that one.

Anyway – I digress! Back home from Scotland we are forced to have *the* conversation that we've been putting off all this time. As I've said, there comes a point though when you realise that perhaps you've had your last curtain call. It felt sad but we had to be realistic; our days of being full-time professional performers were over. The country is overrun with so-called reality shows and talent shows – you know the ones – where *everybody* has talent, or thinks they have ... There are no venues open for real, live cabaret anymore. Even though there are still a whole bunch of really talented, capable magicians out there, who we greatly admire and respect for their unique magical skills – we know few people give a shit. Everybody's life revolves around their fucking flat-screen, HD, 3-D TV now – and unless you're on TV nobody will ever get to hear about you. And you can't possibly be any good *unless you've been on TV right?* This sounds bitter, but it is the bitter truth. This is what 'entertainment' has become and it is the only thing that the public want.

Which brings me to this point in our story; Britain's Got Talent. I cannot tell you everything I know about this show, I can only tell you about our own experience and our feelings and opinions of what happened to us. But I think you will definitely be interested in what I have to say next.

Chapter 28

Let me tell you straight up that we *did not* call this show. Why would we? I think you've worked out that these types of shows are everything we hate about modern entertainment. But the phone rings one day and it's the researcher/producers of Britain's Got Talent. They've discovered our website, they say, and would like us to appear on the show, scheduled for 2008. I tell them no, and in fact refuse the invitation many times in the next few weeks. But they keep calling. They tell me that yes, the programme is mainly made up of amateurs, but that they would like to feature a professional act like ours – as they feel it would enhance the show, as well as our own reputation as professional performers.

This was before the word 'fixed' became associated with these programmes. And unlike now, when everything is blasted across the papers, and all the shenanigans of these shows have been exposed – people really believed in the early days that these were genuine shows looking for hidden talent. A bit like 'New Faces' of the good old days.

As I've said, I cannot tell you everything that I know, but I will tell you what happened to us.

We have now established that I was approached by Britain's Got Talent, not the other way around. Once we had their assurance that they would look after us, we decide to go for it. We had a professional standing of many years, and believed that this was what the show had recognised in us. But they still had certain requirements; they wanted us to be different and they wanted us to be able to set-up quickly between sets – which as you know can present a problem for a good illusionist, because of the type of props that we need. But we were sure we could adapt one of our previous illusions and still have the same level of success with it. Then there was the matter of image – which is often more important than the actual act itself – particularly these days. We steer clear of the sort of outfits we could get away with wearing a few years ago – particularly Claudine – and choose a little number for her that looks feminine and pretty, not raunchy! We put this together with thick dancer's tights, not fishnets – bearing in mind also that this is a family show. It has a lovely burlesque feel to it and we are pleased with the result.

As regards our act – we decide to go with a variation of the pyramid illusion that we have used before, using a very small basket placed on a table. Claudine – now dressed in this beautiful outfit – sensually curls herself into the basket as I dramatically thrust various swords and fire poles through it. It is an illusion we have performed many times, to rapturous response and without sounding too arrogant – we know we are probably one of the best at it. We feel confident that this will work really well on TV.

BGT obviously want to see a full demonstration of the illusion before the show, so we go to London to perform our act – which incidentally is also filmed.

We are invited then to appear at the Hackney Empire in front of thousands of people, and of course, the judges. Simon Cowell says of our performance that 'We have all seen this sort of stuff before,' but that 'The chemistry between us is red hot.' Piers Morgan doesn't object and agrees saying that that's what he liked about our presentation. Amanda Holden hates everything about us. They make this sound, to all intents and purposes, like this is the first time they've seen our act and that their comments and observations are spontaneous. Wrong. Their quips are too rehearsed – and I get the feeling they've definitely seen the film of our act, or at least been told about it by the producers. Either way – we have no idea how this is going to come across on TV – but what we do see is that they're very clever – and that they've created the drama they need for the show when it goes out 'live' in a few months' time.

A few months later we get the call that says we are now definitely part of the semi-final show, which means we will be on TV for a second time. 'How do I *feel*?' they ask me, 'Am I excited?' They tell me the show will change my life. A few days later I am asked what I will be presenting for the semi-final and am invited to attend a meeting, along with the other 39 semi-finalists, to discuss what our second act will consist of.

One-by-one we are all called for a quick meeting with the producer, which is in a private room in the Café de Paris in Regent Street, London. The producer calls me in and proceeds to tell me, 'Fuck Paul Daniels, he's boring and definitely yesterday's news' – *his words*, not mine. He tells me that he liked our sensual spot the first time around, with the 'cooking pot' (I think you remember it was a basket?) and he wants to see this sort of thing again. He's seen an illusion that he likes from one of my old DVDs and wants me to present this for the second spot – he says it would fit in with the 'risqué' feel from before. I wasn't aware that we were being 'risqué' – but I put this slightly strange description to the back of my mind.

The immediate problem here is that we no longer have that illusion as it caused so much bruising for Claudine, so we got rid of it. I have no idea how to even describe it – it was a brilliant illusion, but looked like an instrument of torture – which wasn't far off the truth. But he is adamant and suggests that if we come up with a budget to re-make this illusion – they may be able to pay for it. I'm still not sure and suggest we use my original candle and chandelier act – which I admit is smaller – but it is classy and plays very well, and demonstrates the skill aspect of the magic. He makes it quite clear he doesn't want this. So I suggest another illusion – one that uses levitation. It involves Claudine appearing to float on jets of water, which is incredible to watch in itself, but when the water is turned off she continues to float, rising above and around my head. It has the sensuality that the producer insists he wants and is a very beautiful and classy illusion to present on television. This prop comes at a price though, around £9000, but I'm prepared to pay for it myself because of the importance of this appearance. The conversation ends there though, with no decision having really been reached about our second act, the budget or the funding.

A few days go by and we hear nothing from BGT, so we start phoning them at regular intervals to speak to them about the final decision for using one of these illusions. As I've said I was prepared to pay for the levitation illusion, but not the one the producer had seen on my DVD and was adamant we use – we'd already got rid of it once so we weren't going to pay out to have it built again – only to have to discard it the minute the show was over. But it seemed like nobody wanted to confirm that either one of the illusions were acceptable or that there was any system in place to help fund the building of the prop – so we didn't know which one to go for. They just kept saying that we can't go deciding for ourselves what props we were going to use – we had to get confirmation from the producers first – but the producers wouldn't give us confirmation! Weeks are going by now and every time we call we're getting the same old excuses; they're in meetings or whatever. They just don't seem to understand the urgency of the situation – we've got to start building one or the other of these illusions – and right now! We start to feel that they are deliberately stalling. We have no idea why. We then hear that a number of acts are already being helped by BGT with their semi-final spots. What the hell is going on? After a few more weeks of this we make the decision for ourselves; we will proceed with the levitation illusion.

We visit an illusion builder based in Leicestershire. He boasts on his website that he is an expert in levitation type illusions and is in fact promoting the very prop we need. He is keen to make reference to several top-name professionals he claims he has built this kind of illusion for. He can certainly talk the talk and is indeed, very charming, and we have no doubt that he is the man for the job. A large deposit is paid and work starts. But further visits leave us feeling that perhaps he doesn't really know what he is talking about. In truth though, we're still not sure – all we know is that we need this prop – and fast. I can't disclose the amazing secrets of this illusion, as I believe magic should be protected and kept secret – but when we ask him how he plans to achieve the effect that this illusion requires – he blinds us with the technical specifics of this illusion, again convincing us that he knows what he's doing and we hand over more cash. This is all becoming very stressful as the May 2008 date is looming. BGT has learned by now that we will be using the levitation illusion and they don't seem happy, in fact they seem shocked that we went ahead with building it without their permission. I tell them we had no choice, time was running out and they still hadn't managed to give their permission – so we had to make our own decision.

Finally the prop is delivered to our house, but actually goes up in flames when we rehearse with it. It is immediately returned and the builder is insistent that he can repair it. But by now we have seen that this prop is most definitely not a professional standard working prop. We give him the option to build a much simpler one, but he refuses. We are at our wits end by now; the live semi-finals are just a few weeks away. We are forced to admit defeat with both this prop and its incompetent builder. But what on earth are we supposed to do now? BGT tell us that they are sending a two-man film crew to record our act at a local venue, so that they can see some rough footage of what we have planned. We have nothing planned! We decide to go with our original classy candle and chandelier act – but this is quite a long act and we will have to condense it down to a maximum of one minute, 40 seconds. We rehearse like crazy, honing every move until we get it down to the required time. Although the camera crew are not the decision makers, mores the pity, they love the act and tell us it looks great – it'll be a great spot for the semis. We breathe a sigh of relief.

We are then told in no uncertain terms by BGT that if the press, including local radio stations, get in touch with us – that we are not permitted to speak to them about ourselves, our acts or the show. This is strange. Because we see that a number of the other acts are getting big coverage both in the media and on TV. We come to the conclusion that this can only have been arranged by BGT themselves, as they have their own PR department. We don't know what to make of this, but agree to their terms.

By this point the show has been running for many weeks on TV and we have reached the last week of the series, where our first act with the basket illusion will be seen and we now sit down to watch us on the show.

We cannot believe what we are seeing. The film clip is no longer than about a minute and a half in length but it is made up mainly of Claudine. Her sensual walk onto stage and her disappearing into and emerging from the basket in reality takes no more than 30 seconds – but they have focused almost entirely on this. Even using a clever camera angle to show her bottom as her lacy burlesque-style dress slides up slightly when I lift her from the table at the end of the act. This is cut using shocked expressions on the faces of women in the audience – and excludes the best part of the illusion – the swords and the fire poles entering the basket. They have shown these only in micro-second flashes. The whole thing has a seedy feel to it – something that it most definitely is not. And as for the judges' comments – you already know how we feel about the supposed 'spontaneity' of those. We are stunned. We have been completely misrepresented.

We immediately start to see stuff appearing in the press about us. Ant & Dec call us 'Sexy magic' – which is not what we were trying to be. Sensual yes, but sexy – no. We also notice in the interviews that they film and screen – that they only show you talking about yourselves – when in actual fact you are only answering questions that the judges or Ant & Dec have asked you. But again, very cleverly, they don't screen the questions. We are just seen to be saying for instance 'We have always had a sensual chemistry' – when in fact we've just answered the question 'Tell us why your act is sensual?' This is not something I would ever have said had I not been asked the question – but you simply cannot ignore the question – you're being filmed for God's sake. It's awful. Then we notice that every single article printed in the papers refers not only to our 'Sexy magic' but also mentions our ages and that the fact that we are married, asking ' … is this the last chance saloon' for us?! Madonna recently said in the tabloids that when they start mentioning your age before your name, then you've already lost half the battle. So there you go – that's exactly what I'm trying to say. You will never win when you're up against producers who are 50 steps ahead of you and in charge of editing these shows. Most people's brains, and I'm sorry if this seems harsh – but they appear to be half-dead – which is why they'll believe anything they see on TV – and the producers know this, which is why they keep doing what they do. And it's so wrong.

Two days before the semi-final is filmed, it's agreed that we can use the candle and chandelier act. *Two days*. It's a good job we're professionals and know how to put on a good act under extreme pressure. We give this performance a bit of a gothic twist – but there are no sacrifices or piercings – it is very subtle. We head over to Wembley, where the semi-final will be filmed. There are bits now that I simply cannot discuss, but suffice to say – we have this awful sense of foreboding that we are most definitely being set up. This suddenly gets stronger when I am told that Paul Daniels will be coming to the live finals. (*'Fuck Paul Daniels, he's boring'* right? Remember the producer saying those very words? So why is he now mysteriously appearing at the finals? I wonder ...) We are not the only act that feels like this – other people are feeling apprehensive too, because of the similar way they've been treated. But we are here now, and it is one day before the finals.

All the acts are now required to do a complete run-through on stage – exactly as it will be filmed live the next day. This is in order that any problems can be ironed out. At one point as Claudine and I are ushered from the stage after running through our act, we are directed by stage hands who point us in which direction to walk off. They point to where they want us to go – over to what appears to be a huge black curtain hanging and we assume they want us to go through there. We make our way over and Claudine steps through the curtain and falls about five feet off a ledge – crashing down into all sorts of mechanical equipment. She screams in pain as her legs and back are cut and scraped by all these metal objects, and immediately bruises start to swell up. She is in agony, and I think that she has broken her legs or her back. Hindsight is a terrible thing, and if I'd known what was about to happen next, I would have called a doctor then and there – and sued BGT for negligence. Nobody ever apologised for this incident – nobody – and there was no indication whatsoever that there was a drop behind that piece of black cloth. But under the pressure of the moment, knowing we were due on stage the next day we didn't say anything. We just acted like professionals and didn't make a fuss at all!!

It is now the next day and the live finals. Our moment has come, and we know we're just going to have to pretend that nothing had happened, even though Claudine is in so much pain from her fall. Just before we walk onto stage we notice a huge screen – which actually consists of loads of individual TV screens that act as one big screen – if that makes sense. For the very first time we hear the commentary as we are introduced, literally seconds before we walk on. This is the commentary that you hear at home, and we were told later by so many members of the public that it was obvious from where they were sitting that we were definitely being set up. Let me tell you that from where I was standing, waiting to go onto stage, that that was completely true. Suddenly, as if somebody is orchestrating the whole thing – members of the audience start booing. Then, like a pack of wolves, the *entire audience*, not just a handful of people, join in until the noise is overwhelming. Imagine that – standing there centre stage, waiting to begin our magic; magic that we've done all of our professional lives – and hearing that booing. But there's no going back now – we begin our act and within no time at all, *all* of the judges have buzzed us, and it's no surprise to us that the last buzz comes literally a moment before the beautiful and stunning illusion with the chandelier reaches its finale. We have no doubt now that this has been deliberately planned – Cowell was in the audience the day before as we were rehearsing and saw us perform several times. He saw *first-hand* the precise point where we produce our spectacular chandelier illusion – and yet here we are – buzzed off literally *seconds* before that point. The audience are now shouting 'Off!

Off!' We barely hear the judge's comments, but we register the word 'Boring!,' and Amanda says in a very derogatory fashion that 'Some things are better left at home.' There is even a vile comment about *wife-swapping*!? Where the hell has this come from? I hit back, saying that a visual performance like ours requires a certain amount of time to build up to the finale – but I know it is futile. The judges chuck everything I attempt to say back at us and the audience are braying with delight. As we walk off stage I am asked on camera what I think – I have only one response and snap 'It's a stitch-up.'

Directly after the finals we are all invited back to appear on Britain's Got More Talent with Stephen Mulhern. But we decide to pack up immediately and leave the studio. When the BGMT show is screened, Amanda Holden is seen to be laughing and screaming a sarcastic comment about us, and Paul Daniels is also filmed saying 'They won't be happy with that performance, they should perhaps retire.' Shame on him. 'Bloody idiot,' I think. Here is somebody, who despite being unfriendly towards me all those years ago when I was just starting out, I had always respected. And yet here he is with his wife talking about us in this manner and making these horrible comments about a fellow magician, and then appearing on other crude reality shows – desperate to be seen. Why? Why do this? Again I will say – shame on him.

One thing I forgot to mention is that a few weeks before the semi-finals, we were called by BGT to a meeting in London. At this meeting we were persuaded by them to divert all contact phone numbers and email addresses through their own prominent BGT appointed agent – as our lives would change dramatically after the show and we might find the media attention too intrusive. They assured us that this would be in order for them to deal efficiently and effectively with these endless enquiries. It all seemed quite feasible at the time – so we followed their advice. What we now realise is that this just made certain that we never saw or heard of any contact made by the media – and that it would be almost impossible for us to contact the media via telephone or email –

because all contact was closely monitored. We also learned that the media all work hand-in-glove with the show – so that our own personal story of our experience on the show and our feelings about how we were treated would never reach anyone. Talk about 'big brother' to name yet another hideous machine of our modern world of so-called entertainment.

Claudine was very ill after the show and developed palpitations and an irregular heartbeat – we believe as a direct result of the terrible stress and humiliation of the whole experience. BGTs appointed agent told us that his BlackBerry crashed on the night with the amount of calls and emails from people trying to contact him to voice their anger about the way we were treated. He said that there were literally thousands of people offering us their support. Days later we changed our email address and within hours received literally hundreds of emails from people all over the world – even as far away as Canada – people who were furious at the treatment we had received on BGT, people who said they had genuinely loved our spot. We were even stopped on the street, most people saying how shocked they were and they were so kind to us. But there were also equally as many people who believed everything they saw and posted blogs that were nasty, and people who felt the need to write awful things about us on various forums and other social networking sites. We felt powerless to defend ourselves. Nobody would ever be able to know the whole story – because we will never be able to tell it. I found that hard at the time – but now I think people would actually struggle to believe what really happened to us on that bloody show.

We hoped that Claudine's health might start to improve – but it didn't. The palpitations left her feeling faint – but the longer term issue of the irregular heartbeat was more worrying. She felt so poorly that I took her to see a heart specialist. The first thing he asked her was had she suffered a recent shock or bereavement? We explained the BGT experience, feeling a bit foolish really – but he confirmed our suspicions that this had caused the biopic heartbeat. We later learned that one of the professional acts had actually contemplated suicide as a result of the way he was treated behind the scenes and in front of the BGT cameras, and our hearts went out to him; we completely understood.

I was deeply saddened and very angry by the injustice of the whole thing. We were rightfully proud of our professional career in magic, and it was truly shocking to be ridiculed in this way. But what saddened me the most was that none of my fellow magicians in the UK – literally none of them – contacted us to find out if we were okay or to ask what really happened. Many of them, in fact, continued gossiping about us, clearly unconcerned about how we may have been affected by the show. These people were my peers, and some of them were even my friends – but not anymore.

I learned that some other top magicians in the UK entered BGT over the years – but were told they were rubbish, that they were not worthy of even two minutes on TV. I know who they are, but I will never disclose their names – the artists themselves keep the pain of their experience with BGT very quiet and I would never, ever expose them.

As for the illusion builder; it turned out he had completely fooled us as to his capabilities. We later learned this from many others too. He took thousands of pounds from me (and them) – but never delivered the goods. I made the decision to try to claim the money back from him legally and I won the judgement in the small claims court. But I never did get any of the money back; he disappeared without trace from his premises in Leicestershire. We did feature in the *Daily Star* though, along with a large photo, under the heading 'Smoke 'N' Errors' – so I guess a few people got to read the story of our drama with the levitation prop – but there was no way they would have printed the whole story of why we needed that prop and what happened next – I wonder why??

I have never watched a single episode of Britain's Got Talent or X Factor, or indeed any of those shows since. The only thing I can tell you is that these shows mess with you. If an artist of any kind is genuinely good – and everyone knows that they're good – and they follow this artist, really believing that they will win – then they're in for a shock. Because this isn't enough for the judges of these shows. They have to create controversy and drama – telling the singer, for example, that their mentor chose them the wrong song – unsettling them and making them appear stupid. It's all about the drama; please remember that, it's *not real*. So despite telling us that they hated our magic – they had to make a success of some sort of illusion act in the future, just to keep you, the audience, surprised and interested. And have you ever noticed how all the acts that appear in the finals of these shows are from strategically placed locations all over the UK – so as to maximise the votes from these areas and therefore hugely boost the revenue collected from these unsuspecting voters who are just desperate to see their man win? Nothing happens on these shows on TV without the full orchestration of the producers – trust me on this.

I would tell you so much more, but I can't. I do think the public are coming to their senses in respect to how contrived these shows are now though and that to protect their own gullibility or to save face they have to say 'Oh, yeah – I knew all along it was all a fix.' People are starting to reach their own conclusions and they realise that so much of the time, these shows are just set up to 'stitch you up.' Perhaps I was the first to use that expression in 2008, but I won't be the last. For anybody out there fixated with these shows – then why don't you get yourself a copy of Ben Elton's book – 'Chart Throb' – it is an hilarious and totally brilliant story of the absolute sham of these reality shows. I am laughing all the way through it. Finally – I am able to laugh about the complete nightmare that was, for us anyway, Britain's Got Talent. Thanks Ben!

Chapter 29

It's difficult to know how to wrap this up really, there is still so much to tell you; so many funny stories from so many weird and wonderful places. As for these so-called talent shows – I can only say – don't go near them, please! Don't risk humiliation at the hands of these unscrupulous producers who only care about viewing figures – they do *not* care about you. You may say that our experience was self-inflicted, that we should never have gone on that bloody show – but as we've said – hindsight is a fine thing. If we'd have thought for one minute that BGTs protestations about wanting a 'professional act' on their program were bullshit – we would have run a mile, trust me. And right at the start of this book, when I said there was only one thing in my life that I wish I could change? Well, this was it – but I can't – what's done is done. In the words of Frank Sinatra – '... regrets, I've had a few, but then again, too few to mention.' Haha!

Right. Enough of all that. I was going to tell you about The Masked Magician, wasn't I? We were cruising in the USA when this programme was screened across America in 1997/98 (it was later shown in the UK), and within days we noticed a drastic change in the audience's reactions to our magic. People's responses went from very appreciative applause to a sense now of disappointment. Or was it that we ourselves were so disappointed? All we knew was that our audiences were not responding in the way that we were used to, and that many of them told us they were disgusted and outright angered by the airing of this TV series.' It was unbelievable! We decided to investigate and realised, to our absolute horror, that this program had blown the cover on how some of our best illusions are done. Not only that, but had been edited in such a way as to make them appear easy – like anyone could do them! It takes years and lots of hard work to perfect and hone these illusions – *years* – and now the beautiful magic of magic had been exposed and changed forevermore.

Of course people know that these clever illusions are just that – clever illusions, but that never changed the fact that they are so beautiful and so stunning to watch. People wanted to be amazed and they wanted to sit there and think 'Wow! How on earth did they do that?' They wanted to believe that what we did was a form of art, something they could lose themselves in for a short time. But now they were being shown the very secrets of our magic they felt they now knew everything they needed to know about how it was done, and they lost some respect for our shows. Claudine lost count of how many people made comments about how 'flexible' she must be to carry out these illusions – these were not comments we were used to or liked. There were a few people left who still expressed admiration for the innovative style and visual beauty of our larger and more spectacular acts (perhaps they hadn't seen The Masked Magician) – but mostly the public's response was negative – *very* negative.

Funnily enough though, people very quickly forgot the specifics of what they'd seen on TV – but even so, now that some of these secrets were out – they lost all enthusiasm for this style of illusion.

I hear rumours that the real entertainment value of magic is soon to make a dramatic come-back, that it will rise from the ashes to become an even better version of its original self. But I've been hearing them for nearly 20 years. It's doubtful you will get the public to change their habits now – it is very hard to get people to return to something that they've simply lost interest in. Every year or so that goes by takes another generation further away from the origins of real entertainment – I'm sorry if this sounds negative – I just feel it is the truth.

So the combined effect of having fewer and fewer places to perform and now having to cope with the public's disinterest too, is that it now seems impossible to succeed with this type of illusion show anymore. There are magicians who have come up with brand new concepts and more dynamic ways to present their illusions, but it just isn't the same somehow. Nothing is the same.

While I'm in the mood for having a right old moan, let me mention another thing that changed everything; the smoking ban. Pubs, clubs and bingo halls have been hit really hard since that day in 2007. Whatever your feelings are about smoking, there is no denying that the result of that ban was that people stopped socialising in the pub and it was devastating for landlords. Club and pub owners simply refuse to lay on entertainment for people who aren't there. They were already dealing with the issue of supermarkets selling cheaper-than-cheap alcohol (although that looks set to change with the new minimum price per unit legislation). But even so – how on earth are they supposed to compete price-wise with supermarkets when many of them are 'tied-in' to expensive contracts for the supply of their booze? Add to that the fact that people could no longer enjoy a cigarette and a bit of friendly banter at the bar – and well – the people just stayed away. They drank their cheap beer and smoked their fags at home in front of the TV instead. Which is exactly where the modern entertainment machine wants to keep you – feeding you bullshit that they need you to believe – because it compels you to pick up the phone and dial expensive phone numbers, thus keeping your money where they need it – right back in their big, fat pockets.

So what about the dwindling few that still try to fight the machine? This year we had the opportunity to see a very rare magic show in London featuring the illusionist, Hans Klok. Along with his excellent assistants, he put on a really fantastic run of shows. It was real live entertainment, in the true sense, and extremely professionally staged. But every review we read, although not negative, took the angle that this was a very 1970s/1980s type of show; a bit tired and dated. The problem once again comes down to TV. The public have been saturated with shows featuring these celebrity 'street' magicians – guys whose 'spontaneous' stunts look really impressive on television; putting their hands through panes of glass, walking up buildings or magically inserting a mobile phone in bottle – but, trust me on this one – *none of this* is spontaneous, it's all about the editing. Once again, clever TV production wins – and the real talented magicians lose. I could give you a whole list of incredible magicians, who I really admire, but you will not have heard of a single one of them. Nor are you ever likely to.

When I started in magic, there was no internet. I couldn't just sit in my armchair and Google 'where to buy good magic.' Or more seriously; find out how the tricks are actually done. Anybody can do this now. *Anybody*. When I was learning, magic was still a cherished secret that needed hours and sometimes months of perfecting. The internet has ruined this and has I believe had a very detrimental effect on our art.

In the 1980s close-up magic was a pre-dinner or after-dinner favour, and people thought it was pretty cool. But it didn't stop them from saying 'If you want to do magic though, if you want to be a really *great* magician – you got to do the big stuff with all the props!,' or if you remember, 'If you're gonna do magic – you gotta get a fuckin' bird, mate . . .!' Well I did get the props, and I did get the bird – and for quite a time – it was great.

Now though, people tend to say the opposite – and my close-up magic is what they like to see; people still love the manipulative skill with coins and cigarettes, etc. Both types of magic require intense skill, but in a totally different sense. Don't think for one minute that it is easy to learn to manipulate these objects whilst being so closely scrutinised. It takes immense practice and discipline. But as I've said, anybody can buy these small pocket tricks now, spend a while practising them and then call himself a magician; but it takes a whole lot longer to become as smooth as silk with a silk, or achieve mesmerising fluidity with thimbles or Chinese linking rings. And with regards to the big stage performances – it can take a lifetime dedicated to magic to pull off these illusions; to achieve the poise and confidence that is vital in order to impress your audience.

Let me put it this way. Say you are a solicitor or a nurse, or perhaps a shop assistant. I put you on the spot and ask you to talk for a few minutes about what you do for a living in front of a few people, say a group of about six or seven. I bet you could stand up and do it, particularly if you'd had a short time to prepare mentally for what you were going to say. But say I asked you to walk out onto stage, in front of hundreds of people, and do the same thing. How would you feel about that? As you step out from the wings you have literally seconds to make an impression, just enough time for the audience to decide whether they even like you or not. There is an awful silence as they scrutinize everything about you; how you're dressed, how you walk. And then you pause to compose yourself before you begin, knowing that they're analysing your body language, your confidence (or lack of it). This is before you've even opened your mouth to speak – at which point they start judging your accent, your tone of voice … Do you see what I'm saying? Think back to how Claudine felt in those early days, stepping out into that agonising level of scrutiny! Even the most seasoned of performers, including myself, have struggled with this on occasion. Not only are they trying to suss you out, you've got seconds to suss them out; hundreds of them! What sort of people are they? How are they going to respond to me? I guess I'm just trying to illustrate the difference between close-up magic and stage performances. Both are live. But trust me, the stage performances are the most difficult and sometimes scariest. I have never had a problem performing close-up magic – if a certain group of people are not responding well than I can just move on. Or like the patrolling police officers, *they* can move on – by running away! But live on stage – wow – that is another world.

Magic has changed and life has changed. Gone are the days when people would dress up to attend a live, beautifully presented show. Now they just want to watch some unshaven, tattooed street magician in scruffy jeans and a T-shirt (or worse – don't get me started on the hideous dress code in this country!) on TV. Or you just get all these weird 'alternative' festival-type affairs where anybody can turn up and 'perform' – really strange I think. Everybody is so desperate to be a somebody that they'll do anything to get noticed – and the public seem to love it. I know I shouldn't speak in generalisations, because of course there are people out there who don't like the way entertainment has changed. But if you take the 'show' out of 'show business' – what are you left with? Just plain 'business.' And that is what TV and all other forms of entertainment have become – just another money-making business. Hotels are as much to blame though. Now they will only book something they know is an easy money-spinner; a tribute band or a murder-mystery evening, even a karaoke night. I think you get my point on this.

For this reason, but not only for this reason, I no longer feel the inclination to continue with magic on a full-time, big-scale professional level. It seems that a singer, however rubbish, can get up and sing a song that everybody has heard a million times before – and still get applauded. But a magician can't get away with doing the same trick more than once without being dismissed as boring – 'Oh, we've seen that before' they say, and walk away. No other form of entertainment gets quite the battering that magic does – why is that? I miss the big shows and the amazing illusions though. But I still love the looks of astonishment on people's faces as I perform a little magic for them; just as when I was a kid – I haven't changed in that respect! People, for the most part, actually still respond well to close-up magic. It's as if they actually remember for a short time that live entertainment is so much fun. And it makes it a whole lot easier as regards travelling – no more huge props to box-up and transport – just a few coins and fish that fit into my jacket pocket. I joke – not the fish. But still I am finding there are more and more people out there who have absolutely no respect for magic at all – and why? Possibly for many of the reasons I have shared with you here. I'll shut up now!

So anyway, Claudine and I decided to take a different course. We wanted very much to keep our magic alive but to be in a situation whereby we are not solely reliant on it for our income; we wanted to seriously scale everything down and be able to pick and choose our bookings. In 2008 we started buying precious metals; gold, silver and platinum, and then diamonds (for good measure!). We bought a very old and beautiful house with a small shop frontage in Northamptonshire and opened our very first jewellery shop. It did very, very well. The shop was beautifully fitted-out, as you can imagine (try and keep me away from chandeliers and mirrors!), and our customer base grew and grew. But we soon out-grew this first little shop. We recently relocated to a much bigger place and are now one of the largest independent jewellers in the Midlands. Finally life has settled down – it is being good to us! We've had our little ups and downs of course, but they are always small tribulations – not the life-threatening, lunatic-level tribulations of before! Every now and again we get a little dose of madness – it wouldn't feel like our lives without that – but for the most part our lives are calm and stress-free now. No more toilets in the middle of rooms and skanky mattresses on the floor. Or women pressing their breasts against windows or Japanese men showing you their testicles . . . you don't really get that sort of behaviour in these parts – shame really. Haha! Those events had a special charm all of their own!

So although we are enduring one of the hardest financial situations of our time – unprecedented even – it brings us great pleasure to have succeeded with our new business venture. It makes me smile that all those years ago, at aged just fifteen, I was so in awe of all those guys in Holland in their sharp suits and diamonds, and now here I am – in a sharp suit selling diamonds. Another one of my life's coincidences do you think? And it's funny too that when I used to visit all those businesses the old guys would ask me to show them some magic – and yet here I am years later showing customers a little magic in my own shop. I love that. But in quieter moments, I have to admit that when I sit and reflect on how my life has changed, I sometimes miss the profession that we gave our whole life to, but which now offers us no future.

Chapter 30

I'M STILL PERFORMING magic though – try and stop me! Just on a much, much smaller scale. We came up with the name 'Le Magician Illuminaire' – which I think reflects not only our love of France but suggests a more European feel to our magic. It is representative of how our act has changed too – using the beautiful smaller illusions that feature flames and light. But would you believe that just as people were struggling with the apparent tongue twister that was 'Carl Dean & Claudine' – this time they are struggling to spell Le Magician Illuminaire! Just bloody typical!

As for my fellow magicians, and societies like The Magic Circle, I don't have the same inclination anymore to appear before them. I guess that's because I have been there and done that so many times. But I do have respect for some of my peers who are members of this famous club, and I have always mentioned them in my promotional material. After all, it was The Magic Circle that first brought me to prominence in the magical world.

And I can't conclude without saying a few words to my grandfather. I may have been wrong in my determination to keep you from my limelight, I may even have been wrong assuming that all the mayhem in my life was perhaps you making your point. But I know I am not wrong when I say that I most definitely inherited my passion for the magical and the mystical from you, and for that I thank you. I've met some fantastic people and seen some incredible places as an entertainer. As for all the madness – I've got the physical and mental scars to prove it! So what can I say – lightning bolts and plunging over ravines? The trip over to Jersey and meeting Claudine, the beautiful girl who changed my life. Were you there that day too? Perhaps one day it will all become clear …

In just the last few weeks I have really enjoyed putting on some small shows for people. But I've not been able to escape the inevitable 'incidents!' Why, I ask you? Does this happen to every performer? Don't even answer that – I know what you're thinking.

We were invited to a small company do – just eighty or so people. They'd booked our small cabaret show – perfect. In the middle of the floor was this tall celebration cake; four tiers, all iced and decorated. They were celebrating 25 years in business. Part way through the evening, Claudine looks at me and says those words that I have learned to dread 'Dean, something's not quite right . . .' Well I'm not 37,000 feet in the air this time but I still have reason to be alarmed and start looking around the room with some kind of urgency. 'No,' she says, 'There's something not quite right with the cake.' I take a look. She's right. It has developed a distinct lean. In a nutshell, it has taken on the look of the tower of Pisa. A couple of hours later it looks even worse and as I get up to start setting up the lighting and props for my show Claudine hisses, 'Stay away from the cake . . .' I have no intention of going anywhere near the bloody cake!! But just as I walk across the room the whole thing tilts completely over and splats onto the floor!! The staff and literally everyone in the room looks at me like I have done it!! 'Bloody 'ell,' I think, 'here we go again . . .' Claudine, needless to say, found the whole thing hilarious.

And literally just a few days ago I am booked to do some close-up magic for a wedding. They're an older couple who got married on a cruise (indeed!) but organised a celebration for family and friends when they got back. They have invited about 60 to 70 guests and are really looking forward to the evening. But the weather is horrific; torrential rain and very cold. We discuss the fact that not all the guests may arrive. But do you want to know how many people actually turned up? 12. Yep – 12 people out of a possible 70. And out of that 12 – four told us immediately they hate magic, so we're down to an audience of eight. Out of the eight that are left – two are deaf and two are practically blind. So that brings us to four. And one of these four (I swear, I'm not making this up) – is a woman who looks really crazy and is a bit tipsy. And guess what . . . she tells me she's been on Britain's Got Talent, got buzzed and booed, but seems genuinely happy with her two minutes of fame!

If that doesn't leave you *frankly disillusioned*, then nothing will ...!

A recent publicity photo for our stage shows and website:
www.lemagicianilluminaire.com

A photo taken in 2012 to promote my close-up magic

We are now proud owners of a jewellers shop; one of the largest independent stores in the Midlands. And of course, there had to be a chandelier!

Acknowledgments

To write a book (if you have ever tried it) is a bit of a daunting task. I was surprised though how quickly I got the lines down on paper, and how fast the stories unfolded. But what I struggled to do was bring our stories to life and I knew that for this we would need someone with a very special talent for writing – something I do not possess. Thankfully I knew help was at hand. I know a woman who has written some great articles for us for previous periodicals – all penned in the blink of an eye. She writes with such passion and was always able to capture the real us, I felt. So therefore she was my first choice to help me write this book. Her name is Kimberley.

So we sat down with her and we talked and talked about our experiences and life in magic. And, as if by magic, she brought it all to life. So we are both truly grateful to Kimberley, and pleased that this talented lady was instrumental in writing our book.

***Kimberley LH can be contacted at** morethan_words@live.co.uk*

'Throughout the process of ghost-writing "Frankly Disillusioned," I found myself laughing, swearing, fuming and laughing again – all in a non-stop loop. Just like their book, Dean and Claudine are so funny, so brutally honest and so entertaining. I just wanted the stories to keep coming. I didn't want to have to type . . . "The End." Kimberley'.

www.lemagicianilluminaire.com
www.franklydisillusioned.com
Contact Dean: info@franklydisillusioned.com

Published by The Electronic Book Company
www.theelectronicebookcompany.com

Lightning Source UK Ltd.
Milton Keynes UK
UKOW050900070313

207260UK00008B/209/P

9 781909 465046

RESTRICTED AREAS
ЗАПРЕТНЫЕ ЗОНЫ
SPERRGEBIETE

Restricted areas

Published by:
Manchester Institute for Research and Innovation in Art and Design (MIRIAD),
Manchester Metropolitan University and
The Wapping Project. 2007.

Edition of 500

ISBN 978-1-905476-18-3

Edited by Dr. Jim Aulich

Restricted areas was created with the support of
The Arts and Humanities Research Council (AHRC).

Arts & Humanities Research Council

Designed by AW @ www.axisgraphicdesign.co.uk
Printed by Andrew Kilburn Print Services

Contents

Unknown stories, forgotten places: The photography of Angus Boulton / Angela Weight

Looking at Angus Boulton's work to date, from *The Homeless* (1995–2000) to his latest *08/26* (2007) you are struck by its formal, aesthetic qualities, quite apart from the content. His images are rigorously composed, with an almost classical sense of proportion between land and sky, vertical and horizontal. Colour plays an equally strong role, assuming an abstract quality through the manner in which a slab of red or a blue line anchors the composition. Boulton positions himself in relation to the landscape so that the frame includes quite a lot of foreground – tarmac, cobbles, grass – which in the hands of an amateur would be redundant, but in his work it becomes critically important – a space that holds us at a distance, forcing us to examine the whole picture plane and preventing too much absorption in pictorial detail. Sometimes it acts like a sculptural plinth for a piece of architecture.

The Homeless was criticised for 'aestheticising homelessness', although it won Boulton the *DG Bank Kunststipendium* in 1998, which enabled him to live in Berlin for a year and set him on the path he is following today. But *The Homeless* isn't a social document, even if it had some connection with the artist's own fraught domestic situation at the time. The title is a trifle misleading, since there are no people under the blankets. Rather, this work is an anthropological study of human habitation – even at this most basic level people select their space and construct their shelters. It makes you forcibly aware that people live like this but doesn't invite you to identify with the absent occupiers. The sculptural folds of blankets, cushions stacked up between the pillars of some august City institution, mattresses ranged under a dank colonnade, are emblematic enough of their owners.

Richtung Berlin was the product of the DG Bank stipendium. Starting from the Mark Brandenburg, the city's rural hinterland in the former GDR, he worked inwards through the suburbs observing the city as it was gradually transformed by a stream of reunification money. There are only two photographs of building sites, in what was known for a while as the City of 1200 Cranes, and one of those is hidden behind a hoarding advertising `Lemonbabies Porno'. Within the city, the Berlin Wall had been cut up into re-saleable slabs – one of which found its way to the Imperial War Museum in London, where it stands forlornly in the park – but in the outlying districts sections remained almost intact even at the end of the nineties. At Invaliden – Friedhof it encloses a power station, a mausoleum and the remains of a graveyard. A section has been cut away to allow easier access, while chunks of old tombstones lie about in the foreground. Elsewhere, the blank white walls of new buildings smother and obscure old houses more effectively than the Wall itself ever did. Without self-conscious irony or nudging wit, Boulton gently exposed what his catalogue essayist, Christoph Tannert, described as Berlin's `three radical layers of change: in the system, in the structures and in accepted values.' As a portrait of a city in transition, *Richtung Berlin* is a historical document of unparalleled value, since much of what he recorded nearly a decade ago has long since been swept away by the march of Western capitalism.

However, the fever of reconstruction in Berlin was of much less interest to Boulton than the undulating grassland and sandy forests of Brandenburg, the large and sparsely populated Land that surrounds Berlin. The first five or six photographs in *Richtung Berlin* are of this desolate and

1 / Angus Boulton, 'Film making and photography as record and interpretation,' Schofield, J., Klausmeier, A. and Purbrick, L. (eds), *Re-mapping the Field: New Approaches in Conflict Archaeology*, Berlin: Westkreuz-Verlag 2006, pp. 35–38.

2 / Cornelius Holtorf and Howard Williams, 'Landscapes and Memories', Hicks, D. and Beaudry, M. (eds), *The Cambridge Companion to Historical Archaeology*, Cambridge University Press, 2006, pp. 235–254

mysterious landscape and they form a prologue to Boulton's extensive exploration of the Cold War military bases in East Germany from which the Russians withdrew after the collapse of the German Democratic Republic.

The cultural and architectural legacy of the Communist era continues to be a fertile source of investigation for European artists whose parents' generation grew up in the Cold War or whose own lives, like Boulton's (b.1964), developed during its later stages. But the abandoned Russian bases are largely ignored by their former hosts, while for Boulton they represent a set of values very different to those with which he grew up. As he himself has tellingly remarked, his photographs and films, from *Warrior* to *Kino*, are a comment on the death of a belief system. Looking at this work, it is impossible not to have both admiration and sympathy for what was on one level a hugely idealistic enterprise.

Abandoned and derelict buildings of various kinds are now almost a genre of their own in art and photography, and one may think that one lot of empty corridors, peeling wallpaper and overturned chairs is much like another. Not so where Boulton is concerned. The *Warrior* photographs (1998 – 2007), taken in former Russian bases all over Brandenburg, are imbued with a quite extraordinary atmosphere, partly because these camps and training grounds are lonely and threatening places, but also because they reveal in every frame some physical manifestation of that once omnipotent political creed. The heroic murals that decorate entire walls in many of the communal rooms must have been the work of professional artists, and as for the stencilled instructional figures and symbols in the gymnasia, they put one in mind of Russian modernist paintings.

Boulton's compositional signature, the precisely judged distance between the camera and the middle ground, is used here with great effect. In exteriors, such as the shot of the Firing Range at Forst Zinna, the distance across the sand to the clump of trees, or the target wall just beyond them, is a space our eyes may travel but which holds us at a psychological as well as physical remove. These landscapes with their (deliberately chosen) grey skies were once a performative stage for tanks, firing practice, parades, inspections. Boulton is not some Cold War tourist with a passing interest in the more dramatic aspects of Soviet militaria, but more of an archaeologist: by now familiar with the layout of barrack complexes and training grounds, he explores even their seedy, utilitarian corners and gives them some architectural validity.

The hot summers in this part of Europe permit much more outdoor activity than you would find on a British Army base, and there are outdoor swimming pools and cinemas, one with its ghostly rows of benches still intact, and a circular smoking area with a concrete table and a ring of benches. (Even smoking had to be a communal activity). Isolated in their rural fastnesses, the soldiers had no escape from the dominant ideology. Inside the camp buildings, Boulton positioned himself at the far end of each room, so that the floor, walls and ceiling envelope us like a box. Each space – library, cinema, gymnasium, lecture room - is a container of memory. And he revels in the Russian palette of sour greens, militaristic reds and dirty creams.

41 Gymnasia is a typological subset that came out of Boulton's visits to dozens of former Russian bases. Not all of them are products of the post-war era, as the new occupiers from the East frequently took over pre-existing bases from the Nazi period and even earlier. One thinks of the Bechers' work when considering the formal consistency of these images, but the stripped-out interior volumes and gorgeous colours in which these gymnasia were painted contradict any association with minimalism.

One can't conclude a discussion of Boulton's imagery without some reference to his move to film, which introduces a temporal as well as spatial dimension to his work. His use of sound is naturalistic: silence is interspersed with birdsong, the noise of a train, the soughing of trees, the tick of a Geiger counter, a heavy door slamming, the click of a slide shutter. Near the end of *Cood Bay Forst Zinna* the voices of the Soviet Army Song and Dance Ensemble well up over discarded photographs of army personnel. Jaguars roar out of RAF Coltishall for the last time.

Raking over the coals of history while they are still warm is bound to evoke an emotional response. Angus Boulton does this with a long stick and his critical faculties intact.

Воин – Warrior

11

Организация детей -
это лучший путь
воспитать коммунаров

ПРОЛЕТАРИИ ВСЕХ СТРАН,
ВОИН-АВИАТОР ! ГОРДИСЬ СЛУЖБОЙ В КРАСНОЗНАМЕН-
НЫХ ВОЕННО-ВОЗДУШНЫХ СИЛАХ

Rauchen
219

Angus Boulton, Archaeologist / John Schofield

Artefacts

Angus Boulton is an archaeologist. He may not describe himself as such, and his research practices may not fit within traditional conceptions of archaeology. But for me he is an archaeologist, studying material culture in the pursuit of understanding – picking his was through often baffling and enigmatic landscapes, documenting and attempting to understand empty buildings, and spaces, and the structures, objects and murals within. Like any good archaeologist, Boulton has an eye too for the subtler traces – the small things in which meaning is embedded and through which places are remembered. He captures the atmosphere, the essence of the places he encounters – the auditoria in *Kino*, for example; the woodland now engulfing Stolzenhain; the runways of Wittstock, Marham and Coltishall. His work reveals the character of these places; it gives them an ethereal quality; an enchantment.

And one senses people too. One shares with him the ghosts of place one imagines he must have encountered whilst filming. After watching *Cood bay Forst Zinna*, you feel as though you were there, amongst the occupants – that you know the place, personally, intimately. In *08/26* one encounters people, working at Coltishall, flying and maintaining aircraft – but just as quickly they are gone, fading into the landscape and memory, in the film as in reality. Like any good archaeologist, Boulton is aware of change. His films and imagery capture the sense of decay, documenting the natural and cultural processes by which these places are transformed from homes and work-places, to post-industrial ruins, the symbols of modernity. And it is important that these processes are understood and represented. More than any other places I can think of, these relics of the Cold War, in the words of Tim Edensor, enable us to escape the seamless conformity of our familiar worlds.

Murals

Archaeology is not only about ancient times and old artefacts. Archaeologists now routinely study the contemporary world, and in doing so draw upon a broader range of methodologies and theoretical perspectives than archaeologists investigating the deeper past: film and photography for example complement field survey and artefact analyses in the archaeologists' repertoire. This contemporary archaeology is, by nature and design, inter-disciplinary and very new.

So it is easy to understand how archaeologists and artists come to study the same things, for the same reasons, and often from very similar perspectives. This is precisely how I first came across Boulton. Our worlds coincided over some Cold War murals, in the UK and eastern Germany, created at about the same time by soldiers and airmen serving NATO and the Warsaw Pact respectively. Some murals in the UK were created by American servicemen, far from home, as part of Project Warrior – an official attempt to encourage artistic representation and esprit-de-corps. Some murals were designed to liven up uniformly decorated and furnished living areas and to reinforce presence or 'ownership' within a space. Many of the images reflect contemporary culture and graphic styles, such as comic book characters. As archaeologists we study these contemporary representations just as we do prehistoric paintings on cave walls, representations from the deeper past. These paintings – prehistoric and contemporary – provide coded information about ways in which space is appropriated, used and re-used by a succession of its former occupants. It also provides information on the values attached to those spaces. This approach, archaeologists would say, represents a uniquely archaeological perspective on a significant aspect of modern material culture, within the context of a military culture that continues to shape global current affairs.

Boulton was doing the same thing as us, but in eastern Germany, photographing the murals of Soviet units, in abandoned gymnasia, cinemas and barracks close to Berlin. His representations of these images, though, are very different. Part of this is perhaps their projection and the imaginative use of exhibition space. They look different because of the context in which they are displayed. But they also capture something that other 'documentary' images do not. Because of the resolution, their 'landscape' quality and the emphasis on context, combined with their presentation, one could easily be viewing these murals in situ. They have a three-dimensional quality about them. Every detail of the image, its creation, and subsequent decline can be read in the photograph or film, as it can in the original. The peeling paint, the crumbling plaster – and in his films, the sounds of abandonment, and the conditions in which he found and investigated these paintings: rain, the creaks and whistles of wind ... and bird-song. After experiencing *Cood bay Forst Zinna*, one feels the need for a hot bath, to dry out and warm-up. At *Stolzenhain*, one wishes one had binoculars to identify the song-birds. In *Kino*, I just wanted to sit down and wait for the film to start.

Bases

A further aspect of Angus Boulton's archaeology is spatial awareness. Archaeological surveys usually result in a map: a depiction and interpretation of an earthwork or structural remains visible to archaeologists on the ground. Boulton's work provides no such maps, though one does get the impression of an appreciation, an understanding of the meaning and significance of space. The types of space are clearly represented in *Cood Bay*; as is the size of this settlement. But precisely how one building or room links to another is unclear. In *Stolzenhain*, the landscape is more obvious, and appropriately so, as it is more significant for understanding the base's functionality as a nuclear warhead bunker. Visually representing the site's plan-form is critical for constructing his 'commentary on the art of building for protection'. Boulton succeeds in giving the audience a clear impression of visiting Stolzenhain, stumbling upon it while strolling in the woods before wending their way in from the periphery to the central bunker.

But the absence of mapping is not a criticism. In fact it is a recognition in part of artists leading the way: creating a methodology that suits the aspects and ambitions of contemporary archaeology. Why map contemporary sites like these when Google Earth and other web resources provide this aerial/spatial perspective? Aren't these contemporary places more about perception and experiencing the place, than understanding precisely how the location and orientation of building X relates to building Y? Perhaps it is appropriate that a documentation of sites like Stolzenhain and Forst Zinna comprises a film, and photographs. Perhaps maps are too conventional here? Perhaps it took an artist such as Boulton to demonstrate this – with our formal archaeological training, maybe we can be a little too set in our ways?

1 / Angus Boulton, 'Film making and photography as record and interpretation,' Schofield, J., Klausmeier, A. and Purbrick, L. (eds), *Re-mapping the Field: New Approaches in Conflict Archaeology*, Berlin: Westkreuz-Verlag 2006, pp. 35–38.

2 / Cornelius Holtorf and Howard Williams, 'Landscapes and Memories', Hicks, D. and Beaudry, M. (eds), *The Cambridge Companion to Historical Archaeology*, Cambridge University Press, 2006, pp. 235–254

'Prospective memory'

As an artist, Angus Boulton creates works to be seen today: contemporary archaeology for a contemporary audience. Indeed, the experience of viewing his films is as a virtual visitor. For 20 minutes one is *there*, at Forst Zinna, in that room, viewing a mural with the artist; seeing what he sees, and beginning to comprehend its meaning and significance. And for all their academic rigour, this is something conventional archaeological records rarely achieve. As Boulton himself says:

> 'When artists choose to address sites from the Cold War, it can be assumed that a wide range of interpretations will result, projects that employ alternative methodologies and are undertaken from a somewhat oblique and often unforeseen standpoint. These differing approaches to the question of how and why places of conflict are recorded prove worthy of consideration within an important and growing field of study. Artists are frequently more concerned with the philosophical questions a site imparts rather than the physical nature it exhibits. From a personal perspective, creating photographs and films in such environments provides an opportunity to both inform and challenge an audience.'[1]

But there is a longer-term view, which again draws on the archaeological perspective: that we record, preserve, document and publish interpretive accounts and analyses within the context of what has been termed 'prospective' memory – 'creating realms of memory intended for the future' [and] 'creating elements in [and of] the landscape that will evoke a particular version of a (future) past'.[2] Archaeology is not only about the past, as we have seen. It is also about documenting the present, which includes elements of the contemporary landscape that have persisted from the past. It is also about the future – what of the present landscape will survive into the future, as place or archive, and how will it contribute to understanding the world we have helped to shape and create?

The Cold War is a critical historical period which Angus Boulton and I both experienced from similar perspectives, our fathers being involved in the armed forces. We are of the same generation; almost the same age. We are, to a large extent therefore, on the same wavelength. But alongside us are thousands of other young adults with memories and experiences to match with and contradict our own. Some were the young conscript soldiers far from home at Forst Zinna, one of whom wrote 'Cood bay' on the barrack room wall before he left. Equally are those US servicemen, again of our age, who occupied the barracks of US bases in England, one of whom painted scenes from Dante's *Inferno* on a barrack room wall. There were combatants and civil servants on all sides, and the civilian population whose lives were affected by the political shenanigans of the time.

At the point of writing, everyone over the age of say twenty-five, and living in the northern hemisphere (and some in the southern), will have experiences of the Cold War. That's a lot of memory, an abundance of views and perspectives, most of which will never be captured or expressed beyond the intimate and safe confines of family groups and peers. Where these memories do often find expression is through place:

the fabric and form that gives those memories and opinions a concrete expression. That is why one talks about the ghosts of place, and why we encounter them amidst the buildings, rooms and spaces of abandoned military sites. Angus Boulton's films and photography capture this presence, this sense of humanity, a presence that will always be there on viewing his films, whatever happens to the sites themselves. Unlike the American bases in the UK, these Soviet soldiers, of diverse ethnic, cultural, linguistic backgrounds, and very far from home, will never return to tell us what it was like at Forst Zinna and Stolzenhain. And we have no documents, save the few photos, signs and memoranda on the walls of Forst Zinna. It is for all these reasons that this body of work matters, and why it stands apart. This is Angus Boulton's archaeology.

41 Gymnasia

36

СКА
Perleberg

In his book *Combat Archaeology* John Schofield describes Angus Boulton's recent films as a kind of archaeology.[1] Given the exploration of the material traces of the Cold War in the films *Cood bay Forst Zinna* and *Stolzenhain* Schofield calls Boulton an archaeologist with good reason. In what follows, I do not want to challenge this description, rather my intention is to focus on a particular aspect of recent debate around conflict archaeology: the relationship between archaeology and cultural memory.[2] Defining Boulton as a memory-worker places emphasis upon the broader cultural meanings of his artistic practice. Boulton's work will be discussed as an example of what Schofield defines as archaeology with 'discord value'[3] – archaeology that enables critical reflection upon the conditions of the present.

Stillness and memory

Between 1998 and 2006 Boulton took a series of photographs of different gymnasia at abandoned Soviet military bases in Germany. For all of these photographs the camera was positioned at the centre of one end of the gymnasium resulting in a symmetrical perspective of the rest of the room. The photographs are full of colourful detail, yet highly simple. This format frames the photographic act as documentation and presentation rather than active commentary. The combination of this simple frontal approach with the emptiness and stillness of the depicted scenes locates the gymnasia series within what David Campany has termed 'late photography'.[4] Such photographs picture the aftermaths of violent events and historical processes, alluding to human activity through material remains rather than through the representation of people. Like other 'late' images, the gymnasia photographs are structured by a relationship between presence and absence. The presence of architectural structures marked by human activity and the absence of current human occupation. It is the exaggerated sense of stillness produced by the emptiness of the gymnasia that defines the evocative power and mnemonic function of Boulton's photographs. These are still images of still places.

Although the aim of Boulton's shift into video in 2001 was to introduce movement into his work, stillness is a defining characteristic of his films. The majority of the footage in both *Cood bay Forst Zinna* and *Stolzenhain* is constituted by static shots. The resulting images resemble Boulton's photographs from the gymnasia series. Moreover, the overall effect of both static and panning shots is to emphasise the stillness of the locations explored in the films. Whereas the photographs are frozen moments, the films record the passing of time. But this is time passed without significant event. Trees move and doors bang in the wind, water drips or rushes from drainpipes, unseen birds sing, but nothing really happens in these places. The location is still while the camera moves, and through this contrast it is a sense of stillness and absence that is the key feature of the filmic experience of place. Vilém Flusser has commented that the still camera allows us 'to "take" something from the stream of history',[5] yet in relation to Boulton's photographs and films it is the removal of actual sites from history that precedes the act of visualisation. Stillness is the property of place and not just image. Boulton's practice creates the conditions for this stillness to have meaning.

Boulton's photographs of disused Soviet bases present us with so little in the way of pre-coding that as viewers we are

1 / John Schofield, *Combat Archaeology: Material Culture and Modern Conflict*, London: Duckworth, 2005, p. 79.

2 / Schofield gives support to this approach by committing one of the chapters in his book to the relationship between conflict archaeology and memory. Ibid., pp. 81–114.

3 / Ibid., p. 111.

4 / See David Campany, 'Safety in Numbness: Some remarks on problems of "Late Photography" in, David Green, ed., *Where is the Photograph?*, Brighton: Photoforum and Photoworks, 2003, pp. 123–132.

5 / Vilém Flusser, 'Image and History', *European Photography*, 27:79/80, 2006, p. 6.

forced to either treat them as mute in the extreme, or engage in an active interpretation of place through the images. In comparison Boulton's films are more complex examinations of location involving a sequence of multiple images. The films also involve the introduction of non-diegetic sounds that reinforce the contrast between 'then' and 'now', and enable a more active form of encoding on the part of the artist. At the end of *Cood bay Forst Zinna* Boulton plays *Song of the Civil War* over images of the base at a time when it was operational. *Stolzenhain* ends with the sound of a Geiger counter. Yet I would suggest that there are more similarities than differences between his photographs and films. Both are more records of site than explanatory or critical commentaries. The panning shots in the films are simple devices used to reveal more of the locations under consideration. There is an experiential difference between static and panning shots, but the latter do not move us that far from the acts of simple presentation that define the photographs. The films provide an interpretation of military sites, but within narrow formal limits. As Boulton observes, his approach in the films is 'meditative' rather than declarative and involves the withholding of 'clear answers'.[6]

Confronting such simple and reticent images of abandoned military sites, whether as photography or film, brings us face-to-face with the otherness of the past as something that cannot be grasped in its full complexity. This relationship to the past demands an ethics and politics of reading.[7] Boulton's images have an iconic relationship to the sites they picture and thus have documentary value, but the simplicity of these images also enables viewers to transform them into metaphors for broader historical and political issues. As Boulton comments abandoned military sites are already 'overloaded with metaphors'.[8] Picturing these sites through the limited formal strategies that he adopts enables this metaphoric potential to be actualised as a form of cultural memory.

Remembering the Cold War

Received political history has it that the protracted Cold War confrontation ended with the triumph of the United States. In this context abandoned Soviet military installations might function as metaphors for Soviet defeat and the 'inevitable' supremacy of US led liberal democracy. Boulton's images of the decaying remains of these bases might therefore gain their meaning in contradistinction to images of contemporary military power. Yet such a comparison can also work by contaminating the present with the metaphoric potential of the ruins of the Soviet military system. The question this comparison might raise is: if this powerful system fell into ruin, then why not our own? The potential message of Boulton's work is that there is nothing permanent about even the most apparently permanent forms, whether hardened concrete bunkers or epochal geopolitical systems. All of these are subject to the vicissitudes of time. Here Boulton's images function as metaphors for the contingency of all military orders.

For decades the political imperatives of the Cold War were unquestionable and defined the broad political context of life in Europe and elsewhere. We now live in a different era defined by an apparently endless 'War on Terror'. Like the Cold War, this new framework depends on fear and enmity, and a kind of permanent state of emergency. Bringing this new geopolitical order into a comparative relationship with the

6 / Angus Boulton, 'Film making and photography as record and interpretation' in, John Schofield, Axel Klausmeier and Louise Purbrick, eds., *Re-mapping the Field: New Approaches in Conflict Archaeology*, Berlin and Bonn: Westkreuz-Verlag, 2006, p. 37.

7 / Tim Edensor has made a similar observation in relation to visiting industrial ruins. Tim Edensor, 'Waste matter – The debris of Industrial Ruins and the Disordering of the Material World', *Journal of Material Culture*, 10:3, 2005, p. 330.

8 / Angus Boulton, 'Film making and photography as record and interpretation'. p. 38.

Cold War might allow for the development of a critique of the political and military agendas we are being asked to support. This would involve memory-work that rescues the Cold War past in an effort to produce alternative understandings of the present. Here memory is understood as activity that does not reconstruct the past 'as it was', but brings the past and present together in a new constellation. In Walter Benjamin's terms, such a practice 'leads the past to bring the present into a critical state.'[9] Boulton's photographs and films of abandoned Soviet bases do not entail overt political messages, rather they make aspects of the past visible in such a way that we can re-imagine our relationship to the present through the past.

In his discussion of John Kippin's series of photographs of the former cruise missile base at Greenham Common, entitled *Cold War Pastoral*, Ian Walker described visiting an exhibition of the photographs at Building 150 at Greenham Common in 2001. He observed:

> The date of our visit to Building 150 was Sunday, 2 September 2001. Nine days later, we were again driving along the M4 and turned on the radio to hear that two planes had just crashed into the World Trade Centre in New York. Beyond the windscreen, the rushing traffic seemed unreal and the world uncertain. History hasn't ended – it never does – but it was entering a new chapter and the war of Greenham Common slipped further into the past.[10]

It is precisely this sense of the Cold War slipping into the past and being forgotten that Boulton's work can help ward against. This is a political necessity if only because political rhetoric around '9/11' and its aftermath defined this event as a moment of historical rupture.[11] It is certainly true that new things have emerged since 2001, but has that much really changed? Noam Chomsky stated in 1991 that: 'Viewed realistically, the Cold War has (at most) half-ended.'[12] Chomsky makes this statement on the grounds that much US foreign policy continued as it had for the past forty years.

As this comment suggests, there are significant continuities between the Cold War and the present, something that artistic acts of remembrance might help us understand. Boulton's new film *08/26* makes this kind of dialogue between past and present manifestly obvious. If *Cood bay Forst Zinna* and *Stolzenhain* were entirely focused on the moribund world of the present-past, the new film combines the remains of the military past with the military present. Filming was undertaken at both the disused Soviet air base of Alt-Daber near Wittstock, Germany (the title of the film refers to the runway orientation at this base) and the operational RAF bases at Coltishall and Marham in East Anglia. The film begins with static shots of structures at Alt-Daber – derelict buildings, a crumbling statue of Lenin, the base theatre and gymnasia. A formal shift occurs with the picturing of the aircraft hangers. The camera focuses on the empty space of an unused hanger at Alt-Daber, it then fades into a shot of an operational RAF hangar and back again. This is followed by a close up of one of the abandoned hangars that fades into an image of a hangar occupied by a British jet and back again. From then on the disused and operational are intercut. This fading back and forth between sites creates a shift between the stillness of the present-past and the active present, while also creating a ghostly effect at

9 / Walter Benjamin, *The Arcades Project*, Cambridge, Massachusetts and London: Harvard University Press, 1999, p. 471, N7a, 5.

10 / Ian Walker, 'A Visit to Greenham Common: John Kippin's *Cold War Pastoral*' in *Reviews: Artists and Public Space*, London: Black Dog Publishing, 2005, p. 51.

11 / See Harry Harootunian, 'Remembering the Historical Present', *Critical Inquiry*, 33, Spring 2007, pp. 471–472.

12 / Noam Chomsky, *Deterring Democracy*, London and New York: Verso, 1991, p. 59.

the point of visual transition from one site to another through which the planes and personnel at the operational airfields seem to 'haunt' the abandoned spaces of Alt-Daber. Although a straightforward reading of the film would define the images of Alt-Daber as signs of the past and the images of Coltishall and Marham as signs of the present, it is also possible to read the film as a confusion of past, present, and future. Do the scenes at Alt-Daber so clearly represent the past? Could they not signify the future of the British sites under changed conditions? The shot of the crashed MiG fighter at the end of the film seems to reinforce this possibility.

In this way *08/26* allows us to consider not only the decay of the Soviet base, but also the temporal status of the RAF sites. Through this the film brings into question the relative stability of current military systems. This is clearly an act of memory-work, for it utilises the traces of the past to make meanings about the present. Such work is linked to, but distinct from what Schofield calls 'prospective memory' in his essay in the current publication. It might be possible to detect an element of nostalgia for the Cold War in Boulton's practice, as well as the sense of melancholy that Campany identifies in much 'late' imagery,[13] but his work also presents the possibility for a critical harnessing of what Benjamin termed the 'enormous energies of history'[14] in a politics of memory that is being worked out right now.

13 / David Campany, 'Safety in Numbness', p. 132.

14 / Walter Benjamin, *The Arcades Project*, p. 463, N 3,4.

Films

Cood bay Forst Zinna

Stolzenhain

Kiиo

08/26

Cood bay Forst Zinna

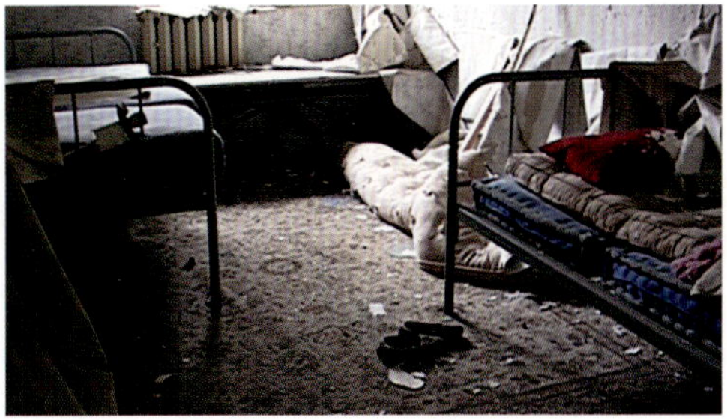

ВЫСОКИМ
ФИЗИЧЕСКОЙ ПОДГОТОВКОЙ, ВОИНСКИМ МАСТЕРСТВО
ВОИН-СПОРТСМЕН

ТЛИЧНОЙ ВАМ СЛУЖБЫ, ТОВАРИЩИ КУРСАНТЫ!

Good-bay Forst-Zinna

Stolzenhain

Z

Kino

В соответствии со
статьей 121 Конститу-
ции СССР создан Со-
вет обороны СССР.
Его председателем
является Л. И. Бреж-
нев.

08/26

СОВЕТСКОМУ

В НЕБЕ КУБАНИ
1943

Encounters / Angus Boulton

1 / *Geschäftsbericht* 1995. Brandenburgische Boden Gesellschaft mbH. 1996.

My father had a map of North Yorkshire. On it, he had carefully marked in pencil the exact location and grid reference of a small number of military aircraft crash sites from the Second World War. One bank holiday back in the late 1970s, we wandered the moors looking for this slightly grim treasure. I recall being surprised that at the head of a gorge, perched on the bank of a stream, we came across the engine of a Blenheim bomber. Further up on top of the moor were the remains of a Spitfire, carefully collected in a swallow hole and still lying there over 30 years after the war. What I found poignant was not the pile of twisted aluminium but the fact that the pilot had apparently died of his wounds before help arrived, unable to move due to a broken leg. I didn't take a photograph because I had no camera but, possibly out of respect, I probably wouldn't have anyway. This was one of those experiences that perhaps explained why for more than a year I would find myself standing at Berlin Spandau station, having risen at 5am to make the 2 hour train journey and four mile walk just to film a disused runway. On this occasion I hadn't left enough time to make the train back, I'd even started running but still missed it by less than a minute. I now had two hours in the cold and rain at Wittstock in which to contemplate precisely what I was doing and why?

Schropp the travellers shop in Potsdamer Strasse had a drawer that contained a large stack of maps on poor quality paper. Seemingly innocuous small single sheets with *Vertrauliche Verschlußsache*! (Confidential Classified Document!) printed in the top right hand corner and DDR on the left. They were unsorted relics from an earlier time when information was only for a privileged minority, now relegated to the bargain bin. A lack of books on the Soviet Military in Eastern Europe meant researching actual locations was difficult. Maps dating from the mid 1980s proved essential and studying them was the starting point for determining sites of interest. Thick purple lines delineated military boundaries, enveloping unusual clusters of buildings and zigzag patterns marking out firing ranges. Maps had always held a degree of fascination, reading the names and imagining the places, but this drawer was quite a find. I'd purchased a large map of Berlin when I first arrived on a residency in 1998, and proceeded to stick coloured pins in it to mark sites while taking photographs for an earlier book on the city. The research resembled a game, finding the bases to visit, initially made all the more interesting because the maps were in German, the Germans seemed to have a limited choice of place names, and there appeared to be at least five villages called Schönewald and Schönefeld on every sheet.

The region of Brandenburg that surrounds Berlin covers approximately 150 x 100 square miles and contained a little over half the total number of Soviet bases inside the former German Democratic Republic. More than 200 installations of different sizes that accommodated around 250,000 troops and additional personnel. Almost all the locations dated from the late Prussian or Nazi periods, and many of the sites and huge training areas underwent further expansion once in Soviet hands. Indeed, over 500,000 acres within Brandenburg had been requisitioned for military use, so that by 1990 around 9% of the overall landscape appeared on maps marked as *Sperrgebiete* or restricted areas.[1]

Layers of history are embedded in the buildings at these installations. Often the gothic script from the Nazi period gradually emerges as rain dissolves the white wash; occasionally it was never painted over, as in the large *Rauchen Verboten*!

warning in red letters at the hangar in Damm. The *Sperrgebiet* itself was to most people an unfamiliar place, a closed off zone where life was experienced away from the public eye. Even after the inhabitants are long gone, many of them seem to retain some menacing aura. I'd been warned about the criminal behaviour and curious types attracted to these areas before signing the routine and often lengthily negotiated four page *Betretungsgenehmigung*, 'permission to enter' document. There were the two men I saw at a distance deep in the woods near Priort: one keeping look out, the other hastily digging. A bungled drug deal at Wittstock that ended in a vicious murder.[2] The burnt out Porsche at Forst Zinna. The skeletal remains of a Russian soldier, uncovered by workmen behind a bricked up alcove. This perhaps illustrates that they had also been desperate places for the unlucky few in the past. Even some of the security guards seemed to treat knowledge as power, ex Stasi officers evading questions as if the answers were still only available on a 'need to know' basis. One crept up on me to check my credentials while I was exploring a depressing officers prison in Potsdam. This warren like building was cold and a uniform dark grey except for the improvised padded cell at the end of the corridor, complete with blood red ceiling. A little later he locked a building with bars on every window at 4 o'clock on a Friday, knowing full well I was still inside. Episodes like these only added to a distinct feeling of intrigue tempered with creeping unease whenever I entered a new location.

The Western Group of the Soviet Armed Forces finally left Germany with the official handover of Central Command in July 1994. Symbolically perhaps, "the last soldier to leave German soil" was photographed by a small group of local press having to hastily jump onto the step of the final military train bound for Moscow as it pulled out of Wünsdorf on September 8th. So ended a chapter in German post war history, the occupiers had finally left. Although the details of this withdrawal can be found in retired officers memoirs and occasionally in a small number of photographic publications, I felt it was perhaps overshadowed as attention in Europe began to concentrate on the Balkans. I recall having seen a very brief news item early in the 1990s showing tanks pulling out of Hungary. But, as the process had taken almost four years, so the media and general public inevitably shifted their focus elsewhere. The actual timetable for withdrawal had been agreed between the Russian and German governments back in October 1990. This would be an enormous logistical task that, despite talk of Kalashnikovs becoming available on the streets of Berlin for 100 Marks, was later acknowledged to have been undertaken relatively successfully after a particularly chaotic start, due partly to a reported 'catastrophic demoralisation' amongst the armed forces.[3] Rumours that cars stolen in Berlin were flown east from Sperenberg are probably true, indeed a Cyrillic sign outside the main gate banning 'the sale of motor vehicles' was still there in 2006. But it was one story from 1991, which finally surfaced in the press in1998 a few months before I arrived in Berlin, that gave a first clue, a name and specific location at which to begin my research.

Greenpeace had plans to secretly buy a nuclear warhead and then unveil it to the public amid fears that a potentially dangerous situation was developing with the perceived threat of nuclear proliferation following the break up of the Soviet Union. A Second Lieutenant accompanied by two soldiers were to bring the weapon out from their base, identified as Altengrabow,

2 / Matthias Anke 'Mord auf dem Flugplatz,' *Märkische Allgemeine*. 2.11.2006. Reported that in February 2006 three men in their early twenties lured Lars I., a local drug dealer, into a trap at the airbase. There he was brutally murdered with an axe, suffered 22 further stab wounds after which his body was doused in petrol, burnt and hidden in a cellar. The trio fled in the victims BMW with 100,000 Euros, failing to notice a further 46,000 Euros in the glove compartment.

3 / Josef Neidhardt 'Ein Heer ohne Staat,' *Die Weltwoche*. Switzerland, No. 12. 19.3.1992. The author reported on Russian soldiers who are selling everything on which they could lay their hands in order to get food: petrol, ammunition, arms, spare parts and their own services. In Moldova a weapons depot was stormed by soldiers, who stole one million rounds of ammunition, several thousand automatic rifles and thirty rocket launchers.

4 / *The Independent*, London 26.7.1998.

5 / Conversations with a British Army Intelligence Officer (retired) between 2000 & 2007.

in return for $250,000 and safe passage to Sweden. The plan never came to fruition as the officer concerned mysteriously disappeared amid the strong belief he had probably been monitored by the KGB all along.[4] One security guard recounted another story, somewhat implausibly, of a warhead 'forgotten' at Neuruppin and later found in a sub basement by workmen carrying out demolition. What I later discovered to be generally accepted was that there had actually been a miscount of the existing nuclear arsenal prior to the signing of the agreement back in 1990, but the Soviet Commanders stuck to their figures and refused to engage with the costly disposal of whatever came to light in addition to that pre-agreed number. Later discoveries were necessarily kept quiet and dealt with either by the German or American authorities.[5]

Wolfgang Weber had first mentioned this forgotten warhead while we drove north from Potsdam on a tour of Ost Prignitz back in 2001. He was an amiable security guard who had been a merchant seaman and consequently his English was quite good. As my own limited German had frequently lead to a degree of disinformation or misunderstanding in the past this proved to be a valuable development. He had later worked with a construction team that had extended and maintained many of the barracks the Russians occupied. Generous with his time and a mine of information, Wolfgang was the only security guard I met who never once asked, 'Why are you doing this?.' Our first stop was at Gadow-Glashütte, a huge bunker complex east of Wittstock that had been abandoned midway through construction. Planned as one of two forward command centres for the 16th Air Army, it consisted of four parallel bunkers the same width and height as the hangars that housed the MiG-29s at Wittstock nearby but here a staggering 200 meters long. The site was half finished because the Berlin Wall had come down before completion, another sign that this event was indeed unforeseen. A thousand tons of reinforced concrete: a Tarkovsky film set lurking in the woods.

There were lighter moments. At our final stop in Perleberg, I idly boasted that I could spot a gymnasium up to a kilometre away, such was my growing familiarity with the architecture and routine layout of a barracks. After wandering ahead I eventually came across 'Perleberg II. 16.3.01'. I peered through the windows, intrigued to have found the most intact example so far and in a previously unseen shade of green. Seeing the door was locked and Wolfgang didn't have a key, it looked like yet another interior that would be missed because the base was scheduled for demolition the following month. As I turned around, somewhat deflated, I caught sight of Wolfgang's colleague who, having eagerly run back to his office and returned fully prepared, proceeded to enthusiastically smash the door in with his axe. The gymnasium had been used as a youth club until fairly recently, tables and chairs set out just like a classroom. They very obligingly moved everything out of the way and I made a photograph. At the very least the building had been documented.

Driving back, I raised the question of why this building had to be demolished, particularly as the visit to Perleberg was only the second occasion on which I had found a building with functioning electricity. Many of these complexes were built by architects who went on to have illustrious careers, the problem lay in the sheer number that existed, and the almost bankrupt finances of Eastern Germany. Wittstock and the huge training area at Schweinrich nearby sit empty, awaiting a government decision whether or not it will become a 24 hour 'Bombodrome', hired out to any nation that has fighter planes and requires a little bombing practice. Forst Zinna was briefly earmarked as a sports training facility. Sperenberg belongs to the city of Berlin, moth-balled as a possible alternative Airport should the planned extension at Schönefeld fall through. The elegant Flying school at Altes Lager, bought recently for a Euro by a Dutch property developer is up for sale again. The converted officers flats that surround it have been comparatively successful and are now, rather ironically, populated by a large percentage of Russian immigrants, but many of the shops have closed through lack of business amid a climate of above average unemployment. Even the spectacular Cargolifter terminal at the airbase in Brand, built by Arups for a new generation of airships is now 'Tropical Islands', reputedly the largest indoor rain forest in the world. Then again, the question of just what to do with the huge structural legacy following the ending of the Cold War is being asked all over the world. This is why 'Robin Hood Airport Doncaster Sheffield' used to be RAF Finningley, where I saw Vulcan bombers perform a three-minute scramble.

I became quite used to hearing the comment "You're just too late" when explaining my project to the few in Germany who were interested. This time it was 'Peter' who was barking it at me, a secretive collector from Berlin. He handed me a sheet of paper from his briefcase, a colour photocopy with small thumbnail images of all sorts of objects he had assembled along with two colleagues, currently stockpiled at a farm "... somewhere in Brandenburg". Here was everything from stained glass windows and canvas murals depicting heroic deeds of the Soviet Military to simple kitchenware; with gas masks and the odd vehicle and uniform in between. But, no guns, he was quite insistent on that point. There was even General Burlakov's red telephone. Presumably, just like the seemingly endless supply of Berlin Wall fragments still sold today, the 'Commander in Chief of the Western Group of the Soviet Armed Forces' once had a lot of phones. I showed Peter some of my work and witnessed his surprise as, apart from a few weeds or peeling paint, little had changed in the intervening years. He also had an envelope containing some intriguing photos of his own, taken while assembling the collection. They included images of rooms with the very same murals I had photographed quite recently, but more curious were the scenes resembling a film set, a dining room with khaki jackets hanging on the backs of chairs, caps and half eaten meals left behind on the tables. Peter explained that he had contacted the Imperial War Museum in London and offered the collection to them. Apparently the curators were quite interested until he named the price, one million euros. Stifling a smile I diplomatically suggested that there simply had to be some rich eccentric American collector of militaria who would no doubt buy the lot, the problem would be finding him.

General Burlakov was brought in from Hungary to oversee completion of the withdrawal following the dismissal of General Snetkov in early 1991, but even he fell under the suspicion of overseeing racketeering, and was pensioned off six months after returning home in 1994.[6] One thought that repeatedly entered my mind while traipsing alone through empty rooms and along endless corridors was where the ultimate destination for the average soldier leaving Germany had been. A question vaguely alluded to at the end of *Cood*

6 / 'Sie haben den Rückzug nicht gelernt,' *Der Spiegel* 10/1991. The official reason for his dismissal was that a colonel commanding a tank regiment had defected to Germany, taking a number of the latest anti-tank weapons with him. By contrast, Burlakov had fulfilled his task and, like many officers, had subsequently become superfluous to the army's needs.

bay Forst Zinna. In comparison to standards elsewhere in the Soviet sphere of influence, Germany was a premiere destination for conscripts serving their two years without leave in solid barracks, as opposed to the possibility of prefabricated huts in the depths of the Ukraine.[7] What became increasingly evident from the state of many buildings following departure were the lengths many went to in order to survive as shortages increased and their future back home became financially uncertain. Anything of value was stolen, sold or reused.

In *08/26* the hardened hangars at Wittstock now stand stranded in a sea of long grass, cut off from the runways. The airbase was occupied and then extended by the Soviet Air Army from the mid 50s continuously until the final flight of MiG-29 aircraft to Damgarten and finally Sernograd in April 1994. The sections of concrete linking the hangars were then removed and transported back to Russia.[8] The German government had provided money and even skilled Turkish construction workers to build accommodation back in Russia as a shortage certainly existed, but much of the money disappeared. Complaints that conscripts were forced to spend the first winter in tents, although exaggerated by an increasingly disgruntled military, were not unfounded. The less fortunate soldiers eventually found themselves in Chechnya as unrest broke out and soon escalated into open warfare.[9]

Frank Gaudlitz was one of the earliest civilian photographers to be allowed to document preparations for the departure. Frank was particularly helpful but it was some of his bizarre experiences that gave an insight into the ordered chaos that developed at times. He had gained access to the local barracks through a little serendipity one evening while on an illicit visit to a sauna in Potsdam. Having failed to notice the two officers out of uniform, a heated exchange took place when their superior entered. Only when Frank demonstrated his tolerance for vodka and a reasonable ability at Cossack dancing was the situation ameliorated. Somewhat surprisingly, it was the same senior officer who organised the permission needed for Gaudlitz to make the photographs that appear alongside this text.[10] What is curious about this series is the fact they could perhaps have been taken at any time in the last 40 years. Frank mentioned how, on returning to Krampnitz soon after the base was handed over, to take colour images, he was staggered to find a handful of feral Russian children hiding in the buildings. Not wanting to return, they had fled when the time to leave arrived and were surviving on the leftover food.

Ultimately, it is the pervasive nature of these damaged landscapes and the stories and myths attached to them that have influenced the photographs and films that I made during almost a decade. Just as a person sometimes struggles to make themselves understood in a foreign language, so by adopting a form of artistic vocabulary as I have, one that is certainly limited, only one small part of the complete story can be told. Too much time spent amid the traces of the past, surrounded by ongoing dereliction, must eventually affect a person, just as military life has lasting effects on those who experience it. As one bemused colleague accompanying me around Stolzenhain, quietly observing the unfamiliar landscape and brutalist structures around her, tellingly remarked: “What kind of paranoia builds this?”

7 / In 2003, the writer Yuri Andrukovich accompanied me to Jüterbog and, surveying his surroundings, almost immediately commented on how it compared with the kind of accommodation he had endured back home in Ukraine.

8 / Lutz Freundt, *Sowjetische Fliegerkräfte Deutschland 1945-94. Band 3*, Edition Freundt, 1994.

9 / William E. Odom, *The collapse of the Soviet Military*, Yale University Press, 2000.

10 / Frank Gaudlitz with Thomas Kumlehn, *Die Russen Gehen – Der Abzug einer Armee.*, BasisDruck Verlag GmbH, Berlin 1993.

Plate list

Воин – Warrior !

9 Parade ground, Nedlitz. 18.9.98
10 Officers Cottages, Krampnitz. 16.3.99
11 Prison, Krampnitz. 16.3.99
"Guard duty is a combat task".
12 Cinema, Krampnitz. 16.3.99
13 Kindergarden, Krampnitz. 17.10.00
14 Office, Krampnitz. 17.10.00
15 Canteen, Krampnitz. 17.10.00
16 Canteen, Rangsdorf. 3.11.00
"Warrior Airmen ! Be proud of your service in Red Army air units".
17 Theatre, Krampnitz. 9.12.98
18 Officer's Swimming pool, Wünsdorf. 1.6.01
19 Helicopter hangar, Damm. 27.10.00
20 Firing range, Forst Zinna. 22.7.99
21 Teaching wall, Krampnitz. 16.3.99

41 Gymnasia

28 Nedlitz. 21.10.98
29 Potsdam I. 23.10.98
30 Beelitz Heilstatten. 4.10.03
31 Jüterbog II. 2.11.00
32 Rangsdorf. 28.10.00
33 Altes Lager II. 10.4.03
34 (clockwise from top left)
Krampnitz I. 9.12.98
Perleberg I. 16.3.01
Forst Zinna I. 27.10.00
Wünsdorf I. 1.6.01
35 (clockwise from top left)
Stolzenhain. 11.4.03
Fürstenwalde I. 29.5.01
Spereneberg I. 31.5.03
Forst Zinna II. 31.10.00
36 Sperenberg III. 24.2.06
37 Perleberg II. 16.3.01

Cood bay Forst Zinna

44 Approach road. Playground. Farm.
45 Bedroom. Gymnasia II. Assualt course.
46 Swimming Pool. Office Mural. Barrack buildings.
47 Gymnasia I mural. Sports club mural. Teaching mural.
48 Underwater tank training area. Library. Unit museum.
49 Podium archive photo. Service flags mural. Graffiti.

Stolzenhain

50 Hohenkuhnsdorfer Heide. Hinterland. Outer perimeter fence.
51 Inner camouflage wall, pillbox. Electric fence, patrol strip. Inner gates.
52 Tunnel entrance. Pillbox/northern sightline. Access trench.
53 Pillbox, observation tower. Bunker escape hatch. Light switch.
54 South Loading bay. Inner bunker door. Inspection chamber.
55 Silo 1. Bunker chamber. Outer door.

Кіно

56 Officers cinema, Forst Zinna. Theatre, Krampnitz. Theatre/Dance hall, Forst Zinna.
57 Theatre, Jüterbog. Outdoor cinema, Forst Zinna. Cinema, Krampnitz.
58 Cinema, Forst Zinna. Brehznev, Forst Zinna. Guards, Forst Zinna.
59 Pilots scrambling, Forst Zinna. Seating, boxes, House of Culture Forst Zinna. Auditorium, Forst Zinna.

08/26

60 Avenue, Wittstock. Plattenbau, Wittstock. Lenin statue, Wittstock.
61 Gymnasium, Wittstock. Forces mural, Wittstock. Museum, Wittstock.
62 Hardened Aircraft Shelter, Wittstock.
HAS close up, Wittstock.
HAS, Tornado, RAF Marham.
63 Hangar 2 Wittstock. Hangar, Jaguars, RAF Coltishall.
Runway directional arrow, Altes Lager.
64 26 Runway Wittstock. 04 Runway, RAF Coltishall. Helipad, Schweinrich.
65 Tornado take-off, RAF Marham.
Hangars, Wittstock. Jaguars, RAF Coltishall.
66 Schiessplatz, Schweinrich. HAS Wittstock. Apron, Wittstock.
67 Jaguars Taxiing, RAF Coltishall. Take-off 04 Runway, RAF Coltishall. MiG-17, Schweinrich.

Die Russen gehen – *Frank Gaudlitz*

71 Nedlitz, August 1991.
72 (clockwise from top left)
Planken, June 1991.
Altes Lager, April 1992.
Planken, June 1992.
Potsdam, June 1991.
75 (clockwise from top left)
Rostock, march 1991.
Kummersdorf Gut, February 1992.
Rostock, March 1992.
Neues Lager, March 1992
76 Altes Lager, April 1992.

Acknowledgements

Many thanks to

Robert Lindner, Frank Gaudlitz, Christoph Oertel & Monica Di Donato, Kirsten Winter, Margrit König, Wolfgang Weber, Marian Kozuskewicz, Jürgen Schmidt, Roswita & Manfred Müller, Mike Barton, Birgit Albrecht, Katrin Röder, Manfred Van Heerde, Enzo & Sushma at Stonehead Cut, Thomas Kemnitz, Axel Schwanenberg, Lina Kim, Michael Wesely, Philippe Van Cauteren, Marie-Luise Buchinger, Anneliese Johnson, Antje Zeiger.

Patric O'Connor, Martin Gale, Angela Weight, Toby Haggith, Katrina Moore, David Low, Niki Michelin, John Schofield, Joachim Scharf, Jim Aulich, Simon Faulkner, Jules Wright, Jeremy Cox, Mick Jennings, Floyd Palmer, Peter Fraser, Michael Dyer Associates, Katrein Günther, Pat & Eric Boulton.

Contributors

Angela Weight has held senior posts at Aberdeen Art Gallery and the Imperial War Museum, London. She is now an independent curator and writer.

Simon Faulkner is a lecturer in the History of Art and Visual Culture at Manchester Metropolitan University. His current research interests are in visual culture and the politics of memory, and in the relationships between visual representation and the Israeli/Palestinian conflict.

John Schofield is head of Military Programmes at English Heritage and a member of the Characterisation Team. He is a Visiting Lecturer in Archaeology at the University of Southampton and a Visiting Fellow in Archaeology and Anthropology at the University of Bristol. He has published several books and articles on recent military archaeology.

Angus Boulton is currently an AHRC research fellow at Manchester Metropolitan University.

Wittstock, February 2006. Photo © Michael Wesely

www.angusboulton.net